International Locomotives

INTERNATIONAL LOCOMOTIVES

From the Collection of Paintings by the late
H. M. Le FLEMING MA MIMechE MILocoE MNECInst

With descriptive material by
A. E. DURRANT

Edited by
J. B. SNELL

Arco Publishing Company, Inc
New York

First published in the United States in 1972 by Arco Publishing Company, Inc,
219 Park Avenue South, New York, NY, 10003

Library of Congress Card Catalog Number 72 184578

© Rosalind Le Fleming and The Institution of Mechanical Engineers, 1972

ISBN 0-668-02639-1

Published in Great Britain by The Institution of Mechanical Engineers

Designed by Derek Morrison
Made and printed in Great Britain

Contents

About the Artist

Hugh Murton Le Fleming was born in Wimborne, Dorset on 11 June 1902, the elder son of Dr Le Fleming, later Chairman of the British Medical Association. Educated at Tonbridge School and Clare College, Cambridge, he was a pupil under C. B. Collett at the Great Western Railway Works at Swindon from 1923 to 1925. After service as an Inspecting Engineer for the Crown Agents, concerned mainly with locomotive construction, he joined the Federated Malay States Railway in 1929 as Assistant District Locomotive Superintendent, in 1931 became Chief Draughtsman in Kuala Lumpur and between 1938 and 1941 was Works Assistant and Assistant to the CME. His health, however, had deteriorated and in September 1941 he was invalided out of the tropical service. This fact prevented fulfilment of his ambition to join the Navy but he obtained the post of Assistant Supply Officer in the Admiralty, being promoted later to Production Engineer. He resigned in 1946 and, never again very strong, died in 1961 at his home in Chiswick, leaving a widow and one son.

There was never any real doubt as to what Hugh Le Fleming's profession would be, although for a time in his early twenties he did play with the idea of becoming a professional painter and living in a garret in Paris. However the necessity of earning a more reliable living, especially when the prospect of marriage loomed up, caused this idea to be abandoned in favour of a career in engineering. From earliest youth he had been fascinated by engines and ships as are many boys, but in his case the attraction lasted and deepened. Very early he knew and was drawing the locomotives to be seen locally and first saw the 'inside' of an engine when taken over the old Somerset & Dorset shed at Wimborne. As soon as he was old enough to escape for expeditions on his own, pocket-money and occasional tips were spent on journeys up the line to spots where, for instance, the Somerset & Dorset crossed the main line from London and a day's good 'bag' of engines could be assured. On visits to London when he was still a small boy his mother, no doubt like many another devoted parent, would spend hours with him at Paddington or hastening between Euston and King's Cross to see particular engines.

While at Cambridge, in 1921, he spent his first 'long vac.' at the Southern Railway's Works at Eastleigh. After the war there had been family holidays on the Continent and this was the period, too, when there began his trips abroad with friends to study foreign locomotives and ships, which, in competition with the pursuit of all his other interests—such as Egyptology and the Ancient World, picture galleries, fine scenery, tropical butterflies and nature study in general—remained his favourite pattern for holidays all his life.

When he obtained his first post on the FMS Railway he maintained that he "must have got into the wrong queue", and certainly he and his wife had been diligently learning Spanish, under the impression that he might be getting a job in South America! His former preparatory school, recording this appointment of an old boy, quipped that it was a job he had already seemed qualified for when he left the school. Be that as it may, the work in Malaya was of great interest to him professionally and in addition gave wonderful scope for the pursuit of some of his 'lay' interests. (He even discovered a new jungle bug that was named after him).

When he was in charge of the locomotive running department of the Northern district of Malaya the job entailed travel right up to the Siamese border and included inspection of the East Coast line, then under construction through virgin jungle. One such journey, his wife remembers, was completed in the dark on the footplate of the engine of the construction line as far as this then reached. The arrival of an inspecting officer from headquarters was bitterly resented by the construction engineer, who arranged that the engine should leave without them on their final day, so that they were marooned and, after a long wait and a slight skirmish with water-buffaloes, only escaped by hailing one of the rare boats on the river.

Between 1931 and 1941, at the Kuala Lumpur (Sentul) workshops, Hugh Le Fleming was responsible for standardisation of locomotive details and reorganisation of the Drawing Office. His most important work in design was the 3-cylinder 4-6-2 engines of 'O' class, the most successful and numerous class on the FMSR and the last steam class to be built. Mr L. Bennett, who served in the Works at this time, remembers also that "Hugh was very keen on riding on footplates to see for himself how the loco behaved and, as far as I know, he was the only 'officer' of our staff who could say he had travelled on the footplate throughout the whole of our system."

Copyright: P. Ransome-Wallis

During the war his work concerned warships and their armament. The strain of those years in Portsmouth and Bath, with constant journeys to armament works in the North, further impaired his health and precluded his undertaking another regular job after his resignation from the Admiralty. The remainder of his life he devoted to painting and the writing of books and a very large number of articles. For financial reasons he took on for a time a series of commissions for the Locomotive Publishing Company, becoming the 'F. Moore' of those days. These F. Moore pictures were large photographs, overpainted in oils and bearing the signature of the original, long-dead Mr Moore. Hugh Le Fleming's writings during this final period included a history of the locomotives of the FMSR, a series of articles on his favourite American locomotives, several sections of the *Concise Encyclopaedia of World Railway Locomotives* and a large number of books on ships, such as *Warships of World War I*, concise histories of the ships of the Blue Funnel and Holland America Lines and 44 editions of the Ian Allan ABC series. With J. H. Price he collaborated in what has been described as an outstanding book on Russian steam locomotives. Having for so many years collected data, planned and indeed started writing a history of Great Western engines he naturally became a leading spirit and one of the principal compilers of the *Locomotive History of the GWR* in which work his technical, Swindon training and researches were of great importance.

All this did entail a great deal of research, pursued with the passion for accuracy that came to be recognized as one of the outstanding qualities of all his work, whether in writing or painting, and by which he avoided perpetuating mistakes of earlier writers and sometimes brought hitherto unknown details to light. This, together with his fund of historical knowledge and the technical background many others lacked, led to his constantly being asked for information and help. It was characteristic of the man to supply this with unfailing generosity, regardless of the time such correspondence might take.

And time, as it turned out, was of the essence, for he died at the early age of 59 leaving more unfulfilled work than could have been completed even in a long life-time.

Mention has been made of his early 'engine-hunting' travels. These continued all his life, with careful planning—not only to see particular engines but if possible to see them working on especially interesting sections —, with footplate passes and permits to visit sheds and works. His 12-year service in Malaya with periodical 'long leaves' provided opportunities for returning home via Japan, Canada and South Africa, besides many more trips to European countries especially Germany. Local annual leave allowed visits to Siam, Java and Sumatra. In 1933 he went as a delegate to the International Railway Congress in Cairo. Characteristically he worked out, for use with his free pass, the longest possible route through Europe. In 1937 came one of the greatest highlights of his whole life, when he went on a tour of his favourite United States railways, with footplate passes on the gigantically powerful freight steam locomotives that were so soon to disappear. As one obituary stated: "He must have been one of the very few Englishmen to have hand-fired an American Mallet locomotive over the Rockies". But little of his graphic and often amusing description of riding on these enormous engines appeared in his articles. Told with his characteristic humour and often sharp wit those more personal impressions enlivened the 'Talks' he gave to various societies or were reserved for a book of reminiscences that was never to get written.

All these travels—including still more to the Continent and one to Russia since the war— not only provided material for books and articles but resulted in notebooks full of sketches and records of engine liveries and scenery, the data for future oil-paintings. He had, of course, continued to paint during the Malayan years— engines, ships, landscapes, even some portraits —besides posters etc. for the railway and other local bodies. Many of these pictures, including over 30 of engines, were subsequently destroyed during the Japanese occupation, together with the coloured sketches for many more. Others, in the possession of friends now

(*continued on page 192*)

PLATE I

Great Western Railway
'Sir Alexander' 2-2-2

In 1873, when these engines were built, standard gauge was still regarded by Great Western diehards as 'narrow gauge', and accorded about as much prestige as the metre gauge in India today—good enough to build new engines for, but that's about all. Nevertheless, with the broad gauge leading the way in respect of size and boiler power, the narrower gauge tended to follow suit, and the Great Western's 4 ft 8½ in-gauge engines were as good as, or better than engines on other lines.

Many, like the one depicted, were of graceful lines, handsomely set off with attractive colours and polished metal-work, and the engine shown here is as reboilered with dome and raised firebox instead of the original flush, domeless arrangement. From about 1882 onwards, they, like so many GWR classes began to appear with all sorts of boiler types, round top or Belpaire fireboxes, domes of assorted sizes and positions, and finally the Churchward type of domeless boiler with raised Belpaire firebox.

Both the 4-4-0, and the 4-6-0 types replaced them as the twentieth century arrived, and most of these 'singles' were scrapped in the first decade of the present century, although one or two remained until the First World War, the last to go being No. 3074, stationed at Taunton.

PLATE 2

Somerset and Dorset Joint Railway
2-4-0 No 15A

This pretty little blue 2-4-0, trundling its train of six-wheeled boxes through a sylvan countryside, was fairly typical of the English branch-line scene in the latter part of the nineteenth century. This machine was built for the original independent Somerset and Dorset Company by George England and Company in 1864. It was a very ordinary small passenger engine and in fact eventually proved rather too small for the S & D's fierce gradients, being sold some years later (and before the S & D adopted its blue livery) to the London and South Western.
But Hugh Le Fleming knew the railway from boyhood, and knew the engine as well; he often recalled with pleasure that one of these dainty Victorian machines was the first he had ever been allowed to crawl beneath, 'to look at the works'. So his painting it in the very attractive S & D blue was a legitimate artist's licence. Probably the engine continued to run on S & D metals from time to time anyhow, since in 1876 the original company was purchased jointly by the Midland and London and South Western Companies, and continued to operate under an independent local management until 1930 with its own fleet of rolling stock (but borrowing as necessary from the owners' stock).

PLATE 3

'American Standard'

4-4-0

So popular did the outside cylinder 4-4-0 with bar frames become in the USA in the nineteenth century, that it was referred to as the 'American' type. In the great days of expansion, when the Mid West, and later the West were opened up to colonists, these little engines handled most of the traffic—passenger and freight. There were, of course, other types, but from about 1850 until the rise of the 4-6-0 and 2-8-0 by the turn of the century, the 4-4-0 was the archetypal USA motive power, as much a part of America as Cowboys and Indians—indeed more so. Its popularity was due to reasonable power and adhesion characteristics, plus (and this was all important) excellent tracking abilities. Pioneer railroads in America were not the heavily engineered and well-ballasted affairs found in Britain. The track looked like two lines of fuse wire nailed to matchsticks, laid straight on to the ground with nothing but earth ballast. The main worry was to lay the maximum miles per day, and the gangs of immigrant labour were encouraged to think more in terms of quantity than quality. So, the crooked lines zig-zagged across the New World, giving no hint of the fact that within a short period of time, railroads in the USA would eclipse the rest of the world in size and capacity, with locomotives having as much load on one axle as this little rococo wood burner weighed *in toto!*

PLATE 4

Paris-Orléans Railway
Group of engines

Monet, painting the extraordinary contrivances lurking under the bridge at the Gare St Lazare would have found nothing to surprise him in this cluster of ancient Orléans power seen here. Leaving on the passenger train is one of the Forquenot 2-4-2 express engines once so popular on a number of French systems. A direct descendant of the Stephenson long-boiler 2-4-0 which preceded them, the trailing axle was added to reduce the 'tail-wagging' tendency produced by the combined effects of outside, overhung, cylinders, and short wheelbase. Outside valve-gear and high running-plates were prophetically modern features in a quaint and bizárre looking design which nevertheless stood the test of time, and lasted in local passenger service until at least 1949, creeping through the wine growing districts under the Pyrenees. Next to the passenger engine are a pair of 0-6-0 engines, that partially seen being the freight version of the passenger design. Also enjoying extreme longevity, these could be seen on light, intermittent duties in the mid- to late 1950s, whilst their broad-gauge counterparts in Spain have but recently departed the railway scene. The third engine seen is clearly a product of the *Entente Cordiale* for, stripped of its Gallic details, the inside-cylinder, outside-framed design is more at home across the Channel, although a number of French lines tried out the scheme from time to time. Whether or not such designs arose out of deliberate Anglophilia, or just happened, seems now lost in the mists of time.

PLATE 5

Austrian Southern Railway
Class 29 0-6-0

A classic from the early days of steam, some of these robust and simple little engines, built in 1860, lasted over 100 years, No 670 of the class, of the Graz Köflacher Eisenbahn, achieving almost 110 years of service.

Two Englishmen, Hall and Haswell, laid the foundations of nineteenth-century Austro-Hungarian locomotive practice, and the outside-framed, outside-cylinder types evolved, with their low boilers and quaint appearance, were long a familiar sight in central Europe. Naturally, the 0-6-0 freight type attained the greatest longevity, being suitable for branch and light shunting work long after being outclassed for main line duties. The standard version drove on the second axle, had inside valve gear, and may occasionally still be seen pottering around the yards of Hungary and elsewhere. The Südbahn, or Southern Railway tended towards individuality, hence this example with long connecting rods driving the rear axle, and the outside Stephenson valve gear. As built they were cabless, and without the unsightly smokebox extension, but otherwise changed little during their centenarian existence – the locomotive shown has a plain chimney, but various types of spark arrester, from 'wild west' diamond stacks to *Kobel* dovecots, have been applied from time to time.

PLATE 6

Great Western Railway
2-4-0 No 1383 and 0-6-0T No 1833

Everything about this scene is redolent of the Great Western—the engines, train, station and signals. Even the church in the background is strangely Great Western, almost as though all places of worship beside the line had to be erected to specifications laid down at Paddington or Swindon. On the passenger train is one of Swindon's 2-4-0 designs, built for ordinary passenger trains, the long-distance 'all (or most) stations' variety, which have now disappeared from British timetables.

Engines like this would work such curious services as all stations from Swindon to Neath via Gloucester, or Swindon—Weymouth. Neath, with its cramped, through station, seems today a strange place to terminate a long-distance train, when just down the line, around the corner, is Swansea. However, Neath was the local divisional locomotive HQ, even in British Railways days, and this probably had some-thing to do with the practice.

Standing in the background is one of a very un-Great Western breed, an 0-6-0 with side tanks. This was the 1813 class, dimensionally similar to the more numerous saddle tanks, and eventually rebuilt like them into the ubiquitous pannier form. The 2-4-0, of course, disappeared many years ago, but a few of the 1813s, in their pannier guise, lasted until BR days.

PLATE 7

Great Western Railway
'Metropolitan' 2-4-0T

For local passenger service in the Southern Division, especially within the London area, Swindon built substantial numbers of these handy 2-4-0Ts. As built, they differed in detail from batch to batch, but all displayed remarkable powers of speed and haulage for such modestly proportioned machines. No. 975 shown here was an early example, and had condensing gear for working in the Metropolitan line tunnels.

Improved cabs, with roofs, later became standard, some even having back sheets as well, although many retained open back cabs to the end. Belpaire fireboxes, and other Great Western standard features were later applied, and the final batch built, numbered in the 3561 series, possessed larger side tanks. Many of the 2-4-0Ts in later years were fitted with the Great Western's own brand of remote control, where by means of a square section telescopic shaft, the engine could be controlled from the leading coach, when pushing a 'push-and-pull' train. Such trains were very modern in concept, despite the frequent use of old motive power, for terminal times could be exceedingly brief.

On many of these 'Auto' trains, as the GWR liked to term them, guards issued tickets, bus style, between unstaffed halts, and there were even coaches with retractable steps, operated by a giant lever in the vestibule, for the benefit of those little communities whose revenue potential rated no more than a nameboard beside the ballast, in lieu of a station.

PLATE 8

Caledonian Railway
7 ft 2 in 2-4-0

The Allan type of double framing, originating at Crewe, became very popular in Scotland and, as will be seen in Plate 15 was built into engines on the Highland Railway until late in the nineteenth century. Earlier, the construction was utilised extensively on the Caledonian Railway, notably for the 2-2-2 and 2-4-0 express engines built by Benjamin Connor for main-line express work. It seems amazing today, that such large-wheeled and apparently feeble power managed to tackle the Anglo-Scottish main line, with Beattock bank thrown in as a major obstacle, but of course, trains were much lighter in those days.

Students of locomotive performance, their thinking often constricted by self-imposed limits, would be surprised to see the result of comparison between the old engines of 100 years ago with the final steam stock. These old-timers often had more power in relationship to their light, 100-ton trains, than later engines. In particular, Connor's 2-4-0s were notably fast runners. Their 7 ft 2 in wheels were, when they were built in 1867, the largest used in Britain: and whether by accident or design their slide valves had unusually long lap and travel, contributing to a freedom of steam entry to (and exit from) the cylinders not exceeded for another 40 years.

PLATE 9

Great Western Railway

0-6-0 No 57

The broad gauge locomotives designed and built at Swindon under Daniel Gooch, were derived from Stephenson's 'North Star' 2-2-2, one of a number of types supplied by various builders for the opening of the line. The Stephenson engines were about the only ones capable of useful work of a strange and bizarre bunch of machinery, resulting from other builders' attempts to comply with Brunel's eccentric specifications, and when Gooch was called upon to produce order out of chaos, he naturally designed into his engines the features which had proved themselves on Stephenson's.

It was no time for experimentation—the original stock contained enough experimental power to keep Gooch in headaches for years, and all Gooch's engines were straightforward, simple designs. One of the striking Stephensonian features adopted was the design of sandwich frame, with its cut-out slots for lightness, and when Swindon was first called upon to build engines for the 4 ft 8½ in gauge, they included this broad gauge characteristic. The engine shown, No 57, is one of the last survivors of these old designs, but is seen here in its final form, with modern Belpaire boiler, and a proper cab. Above the running plate it is virtually a Dean Goods, but below, it can be traced back 50 years earlier, to the dawn of Great Western steam.

PLATE 10

London and North Western Railway
Webb compound 2-2-2-0

One of the strange periods in English locomotive history was the two-decade era of the compound on the LNWR. Not that compounds in themselves were so strange in the latter part of the nineteenth century, just that Francis William Webb's ideas on how to achieve double expansion were curious in their application.

Two-cylinder compounds always seemed lop-sided, with one large and one small cylinder, and four cylinders probably seemed too complicated for a small, three-axle engine, so Webb developed along three-cylinder lines. Now the classic three-cylinder compound with one high- and two low-pressure cylinders, all of comparable size, is an obvious choice, but Webb decided to use two tiny HP cylinders, outside the frames, exhausting into a single 'dustbin-sized' LP cylinder between the frames.

HP and LP drove different axles, which were not coupled, and if that were not sufficiently strange, the LP valve was driven by a slip eccentric, over which the driver had no control. This LP eccentric was actuated by a 'dog' keyed to the axle and crank, and always automatically set itself for the engine's last direction of travel. Thus, when backing down on to a train at a terminus, the LP gear would be in reverse. After half-a-wheel revolution forward, the 'dog' would in theory catch up with the eccentric and rotate it in time for the LP motion to travel forward too, but trouble was to hand if the HP wheels slipped on starting. Exhausting HP steam filled the receiver and caused the LP wheels to revolve—backwards!

Thus, a Webb compound could be frequently seen with its two sets of driving wheels churning furiously around in opposite directions! It is said that Webb was most sensitive about this defect, and refused to admit its obvious disadvantages, although he quietly went over to coupled wheels for his later compounds.

PLATE II

Great Western Railway

2361 Class 0-6-0

William Dean, the GWR's late Victorian locomotive superintendent, seemed uncertain from time to time as to whether he preferred engines with domed or domeless boilers, inside or double frames. One of his most famous classes, the 'Dean Goods', which came out as a domeless, inside-framed type, ended up in the best-known form, with giant domes and Belpaire fireboxes, and included engines 2361–2380 with double frames as shown.

This batch was part of a curious set of standard engines, 0-6-0, 2-4-0, and 0-6-0Ts having standard wheels, cylinders and motion, plus of course, boilers. Compatible with each other, their spare parts were none the less incompatible with other 0-6-0, 2-4-0, and 0-6-0T classes, a typical Swindon anachronism. One wonders whether Churchward, brought up and trained in the joyful muddle which was nineteenth-century Great Western practice, became so exasperated with its peculiarities that he swore to standardise rigidly whenever the opportunity arose. 'All standard but nothing the same' was a common joke amongst Swindon works staff, and while in latter days this was hardly true, it is probably a traditional jibe dating back to Dean days.

PLATE 12

North British Railway

4-4-0T

Whilst the inside cylinder 4-4-0 was a common, almost universal type on British railways, tank engines of the same wheel and cylinder arrangement were a comparative rarity. When a passenger tank engine was wanted, it was usual in the nineteenth century either to reverse the wheel arrangement to 0-4-4T, or to add a trailing pair of wheels to make a 4-4-2T. That the inside cylinder 4-4-0T could be a pleasantly symmetrical piece of steam engineering is clearly shown by this small Scottish engine, one of a number built for light branch-line work. Apart from the pleasing proportions, there is little to say about the engine. It had no effect on current or future practice, partly because many of its tasks vanished with the first branch-line closures in the 1930s; and it had no features of particular interest, although the sandbox ejecting ahead of the trailing bogie wheel will be noted as a curiosity of design.

PLATE 13

Glasgow and South Western Railway
0-4-4T

This rather curious little engine had something in common with the London and South Western class O2 0-4-4T, for it was of a series mechanically similar to, and sharing certain spare parts with contemporary 0-6-0Ts. The two English classes lasted well, the G6 0-6-0T into British Railways days, and the O2, on the Isle of Wight, almost to the end of BR steam.

The engines of Kilmarnock breed, all of them, seemed out of favour with their new owners, the LMS. They were few in number, and therefore non-standard, which always mitigated against their survival, and of course, in early LMS days, anything non-Derby was regarded as an affront, to be eliminated as soon as physically possible. No doubt such an engine, as this, described when built as a shunting engine was likely to have been used mainly on country branches, where small wheels and low adhesion would offer the least inconvenience.

Like many small engines of the British railways, they have been ignored by numerous lavish locomotive histories published in recent years.

PLATE 14

South Eastern and Chatham Railway

Class F 4-4-0

Bedevilled by lack of money, the SE & CR resulted from the marriage of two equally impecunious ancestors, the South Eastern, and the London, Chatham and Dover. With no heavy freight traffic, apart from domestic coal for the human 'battery farms' of south-east London, the SECR was essentially a passenger-carrying line, and a fairly rural one at that.

The most prestigious trains were the Continental expresses to Dover and Folkestone, and there were other important services to coastal towns, and of course, to that bastion of respectability, Tunbridge Wells, served by Hastings trains. Both the North and South Downs were crossed, and these caused some stiff climbs on the main lines, especially the 1 in 53 climb out of Tonbridge, right from the platform end, and complicated by points, crossings, and a sharp curve, leading up to High Brooms: steeper than Shap or Beattock, although not so long.

To tackle this work, Stirling built the F class, and the later, but similar B class, with 7ft wheels and moderate dimensions elsewhere. Rebuilt by Wainwright with domed boilers, as classes F1 and B1, they nevertheless struggled on through the Southern Electric era, and even saw the beginnings of BR's addiction to Doktor Diesel's gift to the Arab nations. Their last hunting ground was the Reading-Redhill line, but here we see an unrebuilt F, in palmier days, ambling through the London suburbs with a train of typical 'birdcage' stock.

PLATE 15

Highland Railway
Jones 4-4-0

In the latter half of the nineteenth century, when most British locomotive engineers were committed to inside cylinders, the Highland, serving the bleak and beautiful regions north of Perth, retained outside cylinder drive. Also the archaic arrangement of partially outside frames, embracing the cylinders and slide bars, and developed from early Crewe practice on the LNWR, still found favour. It looked robust, and probably was.

David Jones was the engineer responsible for these machines, and tucked away as he was, in Lochgorm works at Inverness, he seemed remote from the fashions prevailing south of the Highlands. So remote was he in fact, that after building these sturdy old museum pieces for years, he suddenly blossomed out and produced Britain's first 4-6-0 type, evidently unaware that by so doing, he rendered all the southern lines' practice obsolescent!

The 4-4-0 type, as represented here by No 37, came in a variety of sizes and guises, with different-size wheels for passenger and mixed-traffic work. Most were built new, but others were rebuilt from older 2-4-0 classes. Most were named, and the names reflected their surroundings, for there were the 'Strath' class, the 'Skye Bogies' and many others with names suitably redolent of tartan, and of malt whisky.

PLATE 16

Midland and Great Northern Joint Railway

Johnson 4-4-0

One of the curiosities of British railway practice was the 'joint railway', where two or more major companies combined to operate and own a smaller subsidiary. Such a line was often conceived purely as a means of competing with a third company and where the fruits of such competition were likely to be small in value, a joint line spread the outlay and what benefit there was between its owners. Such was the M&GN, owned by the two Corporations in its title, and built as a raid on the territory of the Great Eastern Railway. Traffic across the broad expanse of East Anglia through which the GER and the M&GN competed, was light—exclusively agricultural and seasonal, and as a result nobody prospered. As on the Somerset and Dorset Joint, Derby managed to impose its locomotive policies upon its semi-subsidiary, although in the latter years of the nineteenth century, before a certain stagnation had set in, Derby's engines were as good as any.

For M&GN passenger work, some 48 Johnson 4-4-0s were supplied by Sharp Stewart and Beyer Peacock between 1894 and 1899, and apart from the yellow colour scheme, they were perfect Midland locomotives. They replaced the assorted 2-4-0 and other engines of the older independent short lines taken over and linked to form the M&GN, and handled this traffic until the railway was eventually taken over by the LNER in 1937. Without the impetus of competition, the line began to fade, and has now been entirely closed, whilst the yellow 4-4-0s have been dead and gone these 30 years.

PLATE 17

Great Western Railway

3001 Class 4-2-2

These fine engines, William Dean's final single-driver type for the Great Western, had the misfortune to arrive just as the railway was changing over, at long last, from Brunel's extravagantly grandiose 7ft gauge, to the more convenient, and otherwise almost universal, 4ft 8½in. Similarly, the turn of the century brought a rapid changeover to 4-4-0s as the main express type; and then, with Churchward in power, these too were soon rendered obsolescent by large 4-6-0s.

The singles, of little or no use for anything other than express work, were soon scrapped. Built thus, in a time of flux, they managed to assume a number of forms. The first 30 were built as 2-2-2s, with a single pair of leading wheels rigidly suspended within the main frames. Of these, eight were turned out as broad-gauge 'convertible' engines, with all wheels outside the double frames. A peculiarly Swindon feature of these was the replacement of the usual running plate and splashers by a long 'mudguard', following the perimeter of each wheel in turn, the end result looking like a glorified 'penny farthing' bicycle! Almost immediately converted to standard gauge, they soon joined their sisters in having the leading pair of wheels replaced by a bogie, and 50 were built new to this 4-2-2 design. Although destined for a short life, many were rebuilt with an assortment of boiler types, and this painting shows a pair of such rebuilds double heading an express train. No. 3060, leading, has a top-feed boiler with raised Belpaire firebox, and the engine behind has an early Churchward boiler, domeless, but with parallel barrel, and no top feed. Both locomotives have cab roofs pitched higher than the originals, and the later pattern of tenders. Had not Churchward taken over, one can imagine Swindon indulging in one of its rebuilding sprees, and converting the lot to 4-4-0s, or even freight engines, but this was not to be.

PLATE 18

Great Eastern Railway
2-4-0 and 4-2-2

The Great Eastern for many years endured a reputation for sloth and inefficiency, although this did not seem to extend to the locomotive department, whose achievements were often of a high order, and certainly up to the usual British standards of the late nineteenth century. In 1885 James Holden took over at Stratford Works, and his first, and standard, express type was a 2-4-0 with 7 ft driving wheels, outside bearings on the leading wheels, and inside frames. In other words, just the sort of express engine as was common in many parts of the British Isles.

Some 110 engines of this class were built from 1886 to 1897, and used on most GE expresses. The invention of steam and air sanding devices caused the GER to build a batch of such engines in 1889 identical, except that they were 2-2-2 single drivers; and then in 1898, came the final singles, ten 4-2-2s with outside frames, very similar to the 4-2-2s built for the Midland, and for the Great Western about the same time. The 2-2-2s had a very short life, and were scrapped by 1907, whilst the later and larger 4-2-2s followed soon after in 1907–10. Meanwhile, 21 of the 2-4-0 class had been rebuilt with larger, higher-pitched boilers, giving a top-heavy look which earned their nickname, 'Humpty Dumpties'. This painting depicts a 'Humpty Dumpty' piloting one of the 4-2-2 singles on an express, probably up Brentwood bank, and represents a very short period of GER history when such a combination could have occurred. Though the 'Humpty Dumpties' were never rebuilt as 4-4-0s, 60 of the remaining engines of the original class were so treated and, as class D13 on the LNER a few survived to the days of the Second World War, the last one disappearing in 1944.

PLATE 19

Great Western Railway
3571 Class 0-4-2T

One of the strange features of the nineteenth-century Great Western was the mutual aloofness between Southern Division locomotive headquarters at Swindon, and the Northern Division works at Wolverhampton, and the inconsistency of the locomotives they produced. Whilst Swindon decreed that 7ft 3in was the proper distance between leading and driving wheels, Wolverhampton chose 7ft 4in, just to ensure that one pedigree could not be contaminated by mixing with the coupling rods of the other. They were even undecided between them as to the best wheel arrangements to use. For general, short-distance, passenger work, Swindon built 2-4-0Ts, whilst Wolverhampton reversed this to 0-4-2T, even though each type was of much the same weight and basic dimensions. Even after the Second World War, fitters in Swindon's 'B' shed referred to the later 4800 class 0-4-2T, built at Swindon, as

'Wolverhampton Engines'!
The last of the true Wolverhampton 0-4-2Ts was the class shown here, depicted in later days with Belpaire firebox, and working an auto-train, as the Great Western were wont to term their push-and-pull light branch units. Small though they were, these little 0-4-2Ts had a good turn of speed, and the last of the 3571 class lasted until after 1945, one being the regular power on the Swindon to Highworth branch.

PLATE 20

Great Western Railway
Group 0-6-0Ts at Worcester

The Great Western had a long love affair with the 0-6-0T type, and for decades they formed about a quarter of the total engines in stock. Few were side tanks; most of those running in the nineteenth century were built with saddle tanks, the twentieth-century engines having pannier tanks. Many of the saddles were later converted to panniers. Swindon and Wolverhampton went their own sweet ways in the design of their locomotives, and even when each works was building 0-6-0Ts of comparable size, power, and appearance, few of the parts would be interchangeable, a crazy situation which was perpetuated under Collett who built versions of each simultaneously at Swindon in the 1930s!
Wolverhampton engines were distinguishable by having a shallower valance angle under the running plate than the Swindon engines, and this basic difference persisted no matter what

boilers, cabs, or tanks were fitted, so that where, as in the 1700, 1800, and 2700 series, each contributed similar engines, the origin could be plainly perceived. Swindon, in addition to the inside-framed type, built two versions with double frames, one with small and the other with larger wheels. The group here looking from left to right, consists of:

1 A Swindon heavy inside-framed locomotive, rebuilt with pannier tanks.
2 A Swindon outside-framed large-wheeled locomotive, rebuilt with pannier tanks.
3 A small Wolverhampton engine, with domeless boiler, raised Belpaire firebox, and pannier tanks. One of this strange variety lurked in the depths of Birkenhead, complete with bell for dock work, until about 1950.
4 A Swindon 'heavy', similar to the first locomotive.

5 A Swindon outside-framed small-wheel engine, still with saddle tank.

Note the variety of bunker shapes, and the open-back cabs, a bleak feature which many retained until finally scrapped under BR auspices.

PLATE 21

Ceinture Railway, Paris
Tandem Compound 4-6-0T

The Ceinture, or belt, railway had, as its main task, the connecting together of all the main-line systems running into Paris. As in most major capitals, each railway ended in a stub terminal, and to connect these, and to provide a local service the *Petit Ceinture*, or Little Belt, formed an irregular loop line, some 2–3 miles out from the main termini. Some 10–15 miles out, connecting the various marshalling yards, was the Great Belt line, the *Grande Ceinture*. Since freight traffic was more important, the latter formed the major portion of the railway, and much of the inner line is now dismantled. However, during the early years of the century, before the 'Metro' and the buses had creamed off all the inner local passenger traffic, the Ceinture occupied a position somewhat akin to London's Inner Circle line, except that it failed to tap directly the important points of traffic. For hauling the passenger trains, a number of tandem compound 4-6-0Ts to this design were built, in line with the Ceinture's exotic tastes in motive power (the line also had some unique de Glehn compound 4-8-0Ts and a batch of du Bousquet 0-6-2 + 2-6-0Ts). These tandem compounds had a variety of advantages over the conventional French compounds, when it came to maintenance and servicing, as all the motion was outside and accessible. On the other hand, balancing the weight of two pistons on a single long rod was a potential problem, although at the Ceinture's low speeds, little trouble in actual practice. Successful and useful they must have been, for they survived to become class 230TA in the National Railways lists, one with a large bunker and trailing truck being 231TA. Four were sold out of service to a local railway in northern France, and, still seeing occasional use around its headquarters at Bapaume in the early 1950s, they can claim to have been the world's last active tandem compound locomotives.

PLATE 22

Great Western Railway
3600 and 2600 Classes

Before the appointment of G. J. Churchward as the head of the GWR locomotive department, Swindon was groping its way in its search for suitable twentieth-century power. In the final decade of the nineteenth century, Dean was still building single drivers for express work, 0-6-0s for the heaviest freight, and 2-4-0Ts for the best suburban services.

Two late attempts to enlarge upon these are shown in this painting, a 3600 class 2-4-2T for suburban work, and a 2600 class outside-framed 2-6-0, always known as 'Aberdares', due to their use on the South Wales coal traffic. Both exhibit Churchward influence in their boiler design, the tank engine with his early, parallel-barrel type, with raised firebox, and the freight locomotive with the later, tapered version. Although they were larger than the older tanks, the 36s were soon eclipsed by Churchward's several 2-6-2T designs. The 2-4-2Ts,

being too big for one- or two-coach push-and-pull trains, were all scrapped during the Great Western's purge of four-coupled engines in the early 1930s, by which time they had been fitted with taper boilers.

The 'Aberdare' freight type was the result of a development commencing with No. 36, a typical Dean double-framed 0-6-0 elongated to a 4-6-0. Looking just like an extended 'Duke', the only radical feature was the use of a wide firebox. She was followed by 2601, a new version with large Churchward boiler having a wide Belpaire firebox with combustion chamber. The old Dean outside-framed bogie was replaced by an inside-framed truck. Ten more were built generally to this design, except that the leading end was supported on a two-wheel pony truck. Entering service at the time of the Anglo-Boer war, these ungainly beasts were known as 'Krugers'. Finally came

the type shown, a 'Kruger' chassis upon which was mounted a Churchward No. 4 standard boiler. Including rebuilds from the 'Krugers', there were 80 'Aberdares', of which 50 survived the Second World War, during which they struggled manfully with main-line freights.

PLATE 23

Great Western Railway
4-4-0 No 4172

Although, as shown here, a perfectly respectable member of the 'Flower' class express 4-4-0s, this particular engine was one of four with an interesting background. In the restless, questing days around 1890, when the cherished broad gauge was being given up for the less unwieldy and more manageable standard gauge, William Dean built a number of weird and wonderful engines quite unlike the respectably conservative Victorian machines he had been wont to produce. Amongst these were Nos 7, 8, 14, and 16, a quartet of express engines which it was hoped would herald a new era.

The first two were 2-2-2 inside cylinder tandem compounds, one each for broad and narrow gauges, whilst the other pair were the ultimate in 2-4-0s, giants with 20in diameter cylinders, and 7ft wheels, built as 'convertibles', ie broad gauge, but designed for easy alteration to standard by the simple process of repositioning the wheels between, instead of outside, the double frames. The first two suffered disastrous mechanical failures and never put in any regular service – luckily these were the good old days when radical new designs were not ordered by the hundred straight off the drawing board, before finding out whether or not they would go.

The coupled engines had no mechanical peculiarities, but were simply over-heavy on the leading pair of wheels. As a result, they were rebuilt as extremely graceful 4-4-0s, and a few useable remnants of the compounds were built into a similar pair of engines. Later they received standard 6ft 8½in wheels in place of the seven-footers, standard No. 2 taper boilers, and were merged into the 'Flower' class, as shown in this painting. Like the other express 4-4-0s, they were replaced in the 1920s and 1930s by the new 'Hall' and 'Castle' 4-6-0s.

PLATE 24

Hungarian State Railways
Class 222 4-4-0

Heading the passenger train out of Budapest is the strange locomotive depicted here, as bizarre a piece of motive power as ever emerged from the dark mysteries of the workshops of Central Europe. Directly descended from the neat, if quaint, 2-4-0 passenger engines building in Austria-Hungary in the middle of the nineteenth century, successive developments had added, in chronological order, a leading bogie, outside Walschaerts valve-gear, and tandem compound cylinders. This was the 222 class, which was built in standard form, to the total of 93 locomotives, and if that were not enough, two of them were rebuilt with Brotan boilers.

This invention of Herr Brotan had, as its main feature, a firebox with water-tube side-walls, thus greatly reducing the amount of staying necessary. At their lower extremities, the tubes were expanded into a hollow foundation ring, and at the top, into a steam drum. For structural reasons, and to provide greater steam space, the top drum was extended over the boiler barrel to the smokebox tubeplate, and was connected to the barrel proper by two or three hollow saddles.

No. 459 of the 222 class, later No 222.059, depicted here, was one of two, from among the tandem compounds which were fitted with the Brotan boiler, the top drum of which was surmounted by a steam dome with spring-balance safety valves, a funnel shaped like a bird bath for filling the boiler, and finally a sandbox, so that the complete ensemble looked like an oveloaded pack mule! Behind the 4-4-0 and clearly from the same stable, if rather less exotic, is a 325 class, inside-framed, two-cylinder compound 0-6-0.

PLATE 25

Belgian State Railways
Locomotive group

Belgium, whilst producing men with such well-known names as Belpaire and Walschaerts, somehow managed to give her locomotives an incredibly clumsy appearance. This curious national characteristic has persisted even into the Diesel age.

Shown here are a group of steam engines thoroughly in the national tradition. Taking the centre of the stage are two of the 'type 12' 2-4-2 Belpaire engines sporting the inside cylinders and outside frames of their time. The second of the two engines also has a triple-barrel boiler, which was supposed to improve the gas flow between the giant firebox and the extraordinary square chimney atop the smokebox. On the left is a 'type 25' 0-6-0 exhibiting features similar to the leading 2-4-2, except that the vast, tapered, chimney is of circular cross-section, and looks like an old fashioned milk churn. Over on the far side is a 'type 6', large-wheeled 2-6-0 used for passenger work through the Ardennes, particularly on the Luxemburg line. The grate areas used on these old Belgian locomotives were enormous, and the 2-6-0 shown had nearly 70 square feet. Presumably this ensured some sort of heat release despite the front-end arrangement, which offends all modern thinking on the proportions of blast pipe and chimney.

PLATE 26

Royal and Imperial Austrian State Railways
Class 60 2-6-0

Into the 'grotesque' category of Karl Gölsdorf's creations come most of the small-boilered low-wheeled engines, such as this little two-cylinder compound 'Mogul'. It is probably the extraordinary boiler mountings which shock most of all, especially to someone brought up in the genteel world of Victorian English engines.

The curious truncated cone atop the chimney is a spark arrester, and even the Austrians had a nickname for this. They called it a *Kobel*, or dovecot. The pipe connecting the two domes is a perfectly sound piece of steam engineering – steam is collected in the rear dome, then passed through the pipe, well clear of the water line, to the regulator housed in the leading dome, thus ensuring a supply of dry steam. However irreverent it sounds, the thing looks just like a handle for lifting the boiler off, as though Floridsdorf works employed giants in its erecting shop! The casing from dome to cylinder conceals the main steam pipe, and appears on the side shown only, of course, for the left-hand side is driven by the low-pressure cylinder, whose exhaust, a measured one-two, one-two, two beats only per revolution, was a strange acoustical phenomenon of two-cylinder compounds.

PLATE 27

Netherlands State Railway
Class 1700 4-4-0

Many railway systems on the Continent of Europe started operations with British-built locomotives, but only in a handful of countries did Britain remain a major supplier for any length of time. Of these faithful, Holland was the closest to the shores of Britain, and her British-built engines were largely constructed at Beyer Peacock's Gorton works. Whether Charles Beyer's continental ancestry had any bearing on this we do not know, but after the old man's death, orders went with increasing frequency to Germany.

Of the Beyer Peacock engines which ran in Holland, the double-framed express types were the ones of greatest classical beauty. First was a 2-4-0 type, some of which were rebuilt with leading bogies, while others were built new as 4-4-0s, such as the one illustrated. Finally, there was a small class of 'Atlantics', the only ones in the world combining the 4-4-2 wheel arrangement with inside cylinders and double frames.

The 4-4-0s, later known as the 1700 class, lasted until after the Second World War, by which time all had been superheated. One of the class ran at one time with hydraulic valve gear, designed by a lady engineer, but little was ever heard of the results obtained in service. At any rate, the experiment was not repeated. At the time they were built, these Dutch 4-4-0s with their outside fly-cranks and polished copper-top chimneys would have looked perfectly at home in Paddington station, perhaps on the 'Flying Dutchman'.

PLATE 28

Great Northern Railway
Stirling 2-2-2s

The most famous single-driver engines on the Great Northern, possibly on any railway in the world (if we except Stephenson's 'Rocket'), were Patrick Stirling's outside-cylinder 4-2-2s with 8 ft driving wheels. Much less often remembered are the same designer's more conventional, and less glamorous, inside-cylinder 2-2-2s, two of which are shown here.

Why two such different designs were produced under the same chief, for the same duties, is a railway enigma; from contemporary accounts, there was little to choose between their performance. The 2-2-2s were the 'ordinary' engines; painted in the local colours they would hardly have been noticed anywhere in the country, whereas the eight-footers were as distinctive in their day as were the A4 Pacifics of two generations later. Built between 1885 and 1894, there were 23 of the 2-2-2 type, and in the double header shown in this painting, the leading engine is in original condition, and the second rebuilt with Ivatt boiler and cab. The train is evidently passing Finsbury Park, after ascending Holloway bank, with the tall somersault signals in the distance already beginning to disappear into the gloom of a typical north London smog.

These Ivatt 2-2-2s were among the last singles to run in Britain, and could still be found on expresses as late as 1913, although all had gone by the end of 1914, replaced by Ivatt's large-boilered 'Atlantics'.

PLATE 29

Midland Railway

4-2-2 Express 'Singles'

After standardising on the 4-4-0 type for express work, the Midland Railway, after a lapse of over 20 years, reintroduced single driver locomotives for express work. The reason behind this was the invention of steam sanding, which improved the adhesion at starting, and was probably needed at times until speeds of 20 to 30 mph were reached, after which the single pair of drivers would give adequate adhesion weight. The first of the new 'Spinners', as the Midland 4-2-2 was known, emerged from Derby works in 1887, and some 95 were built from then until 1900, slightly exceeding in number the similar and equally elegant Dean singles of the Great Western. However, whilst the Dean engines were all the same, at least as far as their major dimensions went, the Midland engines had various sizes of wheels and cylinders, and of boilers. Of the two engines double heading the express shown here, the leading single

is of the final batch with $19\frac{1}{2}$ in × 26 in piston valve cylinders, 7 ft 9 in driving wheels, and double bogie tenders. The second engine is of the previous type, also a piston valve job, but with slightly smaller wheels and cylinders. Like all the final singles, the Midland 600s had a comparatively short life, and were replaced by the superheated 4-4-0s, simple and compound, built by the Midland and its successor the LMS in the early decades of the present century. After being displaced from express service, some of these 'Spinners' were used to pilot freight engines on coal trains from Nottinghamshire to London, on which duties they would hardly seem to have offered much effectiveness. One is preserved.

PLATE 30

North Eastern Railway
4-4-0 and 4-2-2 doubleheader

Passing under a typical semaphore signal gantry of yesteryear, is an express hauled by two of Worsdell's express engines of the late nineteenth century. Leading is a 4-4-0, one of 30 built in 1896–7, with large, 7 ft 1¼ in driving wheels. Two of the same class had 7 ft 7¼ in drivers, the largest diameter coupled wheels ever used in Britain, and exceeded on a worldwide basis only by a couple of freak engines in France. These enormous wheels were fitted to otherwise conventional engines, and nothing of the sort was attempted anywhere for nearly half a century until, in the late 1930s, Germany produced some even more remarkable engines with six-coupled wheels of 7 ft 6½ in diameter.

The second engine on the train shown is one of twenty 4-2-2s built in 1889–90, ten with 7 ft 1¼ in and ten with 7 ft 7¼ in drivers. These were all of Worsdell's two-cylinder compound type, which was supposed to effect economies in fuel. All the singles were soon converted to simples, the large-wheeled ones in 1894–5, and the others in 1900–2. Nevertheless, some good work was got out of the compounds, and one of the large-wheel variety attained 86 mph with a 310-ton train, on level track, producing 1086 ihp in the process. Nevertheless, both single-drivers and two-cylinder compounds are notoriously poor starters, and the combination of the two features must have hastened the conversion to simples. With large, superheated 4-4-0s, 'Atlantics', and 'Pacifics' following each other rapidly in the twentieth century, the singles soon went to the scrap heap, being useless for anything other than express work, and becoming too small for that.

PLATE 31

Great Western Railway
2800 Class 2-8-0

From the days of Timothy Hackworth to the 1922 grouping of British railways, there were companies which never had anything larger than the 0-6-0 type for main-line goods and mineral traffic. In 1903, when Churchward completed his 2-8-0 No 97, the 0-6-0 lines were in a majority, only the London and North Western having a significant number of eight-coupled units. Apart from being eight-coupled, the GWR engine was a modern conception, with long-lap valves in straight-ported cylinders, a freight version of the same designer's epoch making 4-6-0 No. 100.

Whilst Churchward settled his standards, the 'twenty-eights' differed slightly from batch to batch, enlarging the cylinders by small stages, and gradually progressing to the standard No 1 boiler with superheater and fully tapered barrel. At this stage, in 1911, the design was finalised, and continued to serve as Swindon's standard main-line heavy freight engine until the end of the Great Western's existence in 1947. With a further batch built from 1938 onwards, having no other modification than a better cab, the 2800 type could be seen on the Western Region of British Railways mineral traffic virtually to the end of steam, in the mid-1960s.

From time to time, the GWR was invaded by other 2-8-0s, Robinson's Great Central design after the First World War, and both the Stanier and American varieties during the Second World War. None of these was on paper or in practice, the equal of Churchward's engine.

PLATE 32

Great Western Railway
2900 Class 4-6-0

The very first of Britain's extensive range of modern steam power was Churchward's two-cylinder 'twenty nine' class. Derived mainly from American practice, adapted to British conditions, and improved in detail, these 4-6-0s were head and shoulders above contemporary power when built. This is hardly surprising, for the average express engine in the UK, in 1900, had scarcely advanced from those produced 30 years earlier. Churchward, a supreme iconoclast, swept away the prejudices of Victorian motive power policies, and brought the Great Western into the twentieth century with a bang. Boiler development came first, and the final Churchward standard, with taper barrel and tapered firebox with curved sides to promote circulation, clearly owed a lot to the Brooks Locomotive Works, of Dunkirk, New York, where a number of designs with similar boilers had previously been produced.

Churchward, on a visit to the USA, had seen, and been impressed by these engines. Cylinder designs, with large diameter piston valves, set slightly inboard from the cylinder centres, and featuring straight, direct, ports, were another Brooks feature adopted with success. Even the design of the cylinders, each cast with a half-saddle, was purely American, and as these did not adapt themselves to the plate frames of British practice, which gave more firebox room than USA bar frames, a combination plate and bar frame was used, similar to those applied to the von Borries compounds in Prussia. Long-lap valves to improve expansion were used, following both Schmidt's early superheated locos in Prussia, and the first Pennsylvania 'Atlantics', where long lap was applied to *slide valves*. With all these features plus superheating, Churchward's engines were 20 years ahead of current British practice. The

features he adopted as standard persisted through to the last steam locomotives built for British Railways, a tribute to his perspicacity in adopting the best practice seen in the world, instead of restricting his outlook to local usage. The engine in the painting, No 2935, was experimentally fitted with poppet valves, the GWRs only example of this type.

PLATE 33

Belgian State Railways
Class 8 4-6-0

In their constant quest for effective motive power, the Belgians had often to seek abroad, and when the strange native types shown in plate 25 failed to cope with the twentieth-century traffic, five Caledonian Railway 'Dunalastair' 4-4-0s were imported from Scotland. These worked splendidly, and the local Belgian works were soon churning out many more, together with a 4-4-2T version, and 0-6-0 goods varieties. They even built two types of 'Caledonian' 4-6-0s, not the *Cardean* express engines, but the smaller-wheeled mixed-traffic version. However, these were never as good, size for size, as the original Scottish, smaller, types, and the quest turned next to the immediate neighbour, France, for the next locomotive generation.

Two de Glehn classes ensued, the 'type 6' 4-4-2, and the 'type 8' 4-6-0 shown. Useful engines, they lasted well, and were joined later by the 'type 7', which was an enlarged version of the 8, and at first classed 8bis. Later, the Belgians made gigantic and clumsy, four-cylinder engines, and when steam finally ceased work, the mainstay were the post-1945 Canadian 2-8-0s, ably supported by ex-Prussian veteran 0-8-0s from the First World War.

PLATE 34

Great Northern Railway
Compound 4-4-2 No 292

The Great Northern and the Great Western railways were, at the turn of the century, the first British systems to introduce the wide firebox. Popular writers, who for some odd reason, think only in terms of express trains, usually ignore Dean's freight 2-6-0 and 4-6-0 types, and describe these 'Atlantics' by the Great Northern's H. A. Ivatt as being the forerunners of the latter-day fleets of wide-firebox machines.

These Ivatt large 'Atlantics' were a simple modification of his earlier small-boilered version which had a small-diameter boiler and narrow firebox, and no attempt was made to increase the cylinder capacity to suit the larger boiler. Impressed, no doubt, by the de Glehn compounds in France, Ivatt converted one of his large 4-4-2s, No 292 shown here, to compound expansion, with no beneficial results. In their unsuperheated form, the 'Atlantics' were not outstanding performers, but with superheaters, especially the large superheaters fitted by H. N. Gresley, and with larger, piston valve cylinders, some brilliant work was coaxed out of these locomotives, especially when called upon to deputise for a 'Pacific'.

No 292 was the last GNR compound locomotive to remain in service; she was never rebuilt, not even superheated, and was a familiar sight on the Lincolnshire lines until her demise in 1927.

PLATE 35

Prussian State Railways
'Uniflow' locomotives

A logical development, stemming from the introduction of superheating, was that of the 'Uniflow' cylinder, or, as the German inventor Stumpf called it, the *gleichström* system. With the higher temperatures attained with superheated steam, the problem arose that the same steam ports had to deal alternatively with superheated live steam at 700 to 800°F, and exhaust in the 250° to 300°F range. The theory was that hot steam entering ports cooled by the exhaust, thus lost some of its heat to the port walls, and the cooler exhaust steam then gathered up this heat on the way out, and threw it up the chimney. The argument seems somewhat academic, and the likelihood of a large mass of metal, such as a locomotive cylinder, heating and cooling to this extent at the rate of two or three hundred times a minute, seems hard to believe. However, the Germans are nothing if not thorough, and Stumpf devised his system where live steam was admitted through end ports in the usual manner, to be exhausted centrally through a large port uncovered by the piston itself. To achieve this, the piston head was almost as long as the stroke traversed, and the whole concept had much in common with the later, two-stroke, internal-combustion engine. Two Prussian passenger engines were equipped with Stumpf's cylinders, and they are both to be seen in this painting. Closest is an S6 4-4-0, largest and last of the type built for Prussia, and this had an early version of Lentz's poppet valves to admit live steam. These, and the bulge of the central exhaust port can be clearly seen. Behind, is one of the S10^2 three-cylinder 4-6-0s retaining ordinary piston valves. Due to the great length of the cylinders, to accommodate the Stumpf piston, this alone of the S10^{2}s had divided drive, as can be seen. In service, the 'Uniflow' cylinders showed little if any thermal advantage, and the heavy pistons were difficult to balance, so the engines reverted to standard. It is interesting to note, though, that the former Stumpf 4-6-0 retained divided drive, and as Reichsbahn No 17202, was always distinguishable from its fellows.

PLATE 36

Eastern Railway of France
Series 8 4-4-0

Outside Britain, few countries in Europe made any attempt to develop the 4-4-0 type to the limits dictated by the prevailing track conditions. The Prussian S6, the Austrian 306, and these French engines represented the last stand of the type before it was smothered beneath numerous 'Pacifics'. Apart from its size, the design was a straightforward enlargement of the standard de Glehn four-cylinder compounds so justly famous throughout France and elsewhere, and featured slide valves on all four cylinders, to distribute the unsuperheated steam.

The 30 engines were used during the period when other French lines had turned to the 'Atlantic' for their top passenger duties, and until the arrival of the larger 4-6-0 and 4-8-2 classes, these bore the brunt of the heavy international express work from Paris eastwards to the borders of Alsace-Lorraine, Luxemburg, and Switzerland.

Their reign was brief, however, and little has come to light concerning their prowess. Despite an early downgrading, they seem to have lasted into the early 1940s, and as late as 1949 one could be seen, humbly doing duty as stationary boiler at Nancy shed.

PLATE 37

Northern Railway of France

4-6-0 3.539

In the early days of the present century, de Glehn's 'Atlantics' were receiving a great deal of publicity for their performance on French express trains. However, they were greatly exceeded in number by a very useful design, or rather series of designs, of 4-6-0 mixed-traffic engines, of which every railway had versions. The Nord had two types, a small, lightweight class almost identical to the original series 1301 of the CF du Midi, and the larger engine depicted here. This class was virtually the counterpart of the 4-4-2 design, having a similar boiler; like the 'Atlantics', the design was originally unsuperheated, with slide valves on all cylinders. As shown, the engine is superheated, with new high-pressure cylinders, fed through piston valves. In later years, all were fitted with Lemaître multiple-jet blastpipes and large-diameter chimneys and, as class 230D of the SNCF were a familiar sight at Paris until the mid-1960s, and at Boulogne even later.

PLATE 38

London Brighton and South Coast Railway
Class B2X 4-4-0

During the 20 years of the Stroudley regime on the Brighton line, express engines had been characterised by the unusual wheel arrangement of 0-4-2, the best-known of these being the 'Gladstone' class. Probably to many people's surprise, these back-to-front sounding engines stayed on the rails, even when going quite fast, and it was not until R. J. Billinton succeeded Stroudley in 1890 that bogie passenger engines became a feature of this railway. The first Billinton bogies were the D3 class 0-4-4Ts, built from 1892, and his B2 4-4-0 express engines followed in 1895. The engine shown, No 206, formerly named 'Smeaton', was the first engine to run from London to Brighton in an hour, a feat achieved in October 1898, and recorded by Rous-Marten. As shown here, it is rebuilt with a larger boiler, and classed B2X, and is seen painted in Marsh's umber livery. This rebuilt version closely resembled the

later and better-known 4-4-0, of class B4, which with their raised running plates and drumhead smokeboxes gave the appearance of modern and efficient machines, accentuated all the more in the rebuilt and superheated B4X class. It is sad to relate, then, that all was appearance only, and the earliest Brighton 4-4-0s were usually of such a sluggish disposition that they were ousted on the best duties by tank engines!

PLATE 39

London and North Western Railway
'George V' Class 4-4-0

The LNWR often called itself 'The Premier Line', an historically plausible title, considering its absorption of the Liverpool and Manchester Railway, and of the London and Birmingham. However, in the matter of motive power, the LNWR was one of those lines which eventually banded together in 1923 to give the London, Midland and Scottish Railway a stock of the most numerous and least effective engines of all the four new railways. The London and North Western had the hardest duties to perform, in the shape of the 300-mile main line from Euston to Carlisle, over which heavy expresses had to be hauled at fairly high speeds, including the climb each way over Shap summit. It was fortunate that the LNWR also tapped large coal deposits, a fact which must have eased the financial burden of undersized and inefficient engines, throwing vast quantities of unburnt coal out of the chimney.

Until the turn of the century, Webb's curious compounds (see plate No 10) struggled with the traffic, and when Whale supplanted him, a new class of simple, straightforward 4-4-0s replaced the compounds, almost overnight. These were far more powerful and reliable than the compounds, but were shown up quite soon after by a LBSCR superheated 4-4-2T, which was able to perform the same duties using far less water than the LNWR tender engine. Consequently, the 'George V' 4-4-0s were built as a superheated version of the previous 'Precursor' class, with resulting economies.

In LMS days, the LNWR engines were scrapped rather rapidly on the grounds that they were heavier on fuel and maintenance than the Derby product, although at the time nobody seems to have realised that if they did thrice the work on twice the coal, then they must have been more economical than the Midland's pampered pets. However, Derby men were in charge, and that was all that mattered! A handful of these 4-4-0s, four of each class, survived the Second World War, but were scrapped almost immediately afterwards.

PLATE 40

Caledonian Railway

903 Class 4-6-0

As the twentieth century brought with it heavier steel coaches with corridors, dining cars, and so the need for greatly increased engine power, many British locomotive engineers were caught unprepared. For express work, the 4-4-0 had only just supplanted the 4-2-2 or 2-2-2 as standard power, yet further demands for greater capacity were made at once, by the commercial department. The temptation to retain the 4-4-0's inside-cylinder arrangement, add another pair of driving wheels, and hope for the best on boiler proportions, was sometimes difficult to overcome, and the Caledonian's Chief Mechanical Engineer, J. F. McIntosh, succumbed to it. The result was a number of very imposing looking 4-6-0s, some with express-size wheels, some for mixed traffic, and others with small wheels for goods and slow passenger work. Most famous was 903 'Cardean', which, resplendent in blue livery, regularly hauled the Anglo-Scottish expresses north of Carlisle. None of the 4-6-0 classes was built in large numbers, as performance was never commensurate with their size, and higher power outputs could only be attained by thrashing the small-grated boilers, with resultant high fuel consumption. They lasted into LMS days, but the 'Royal Scot' 4-6-0s displaced them in express service in 1927, the Hughes 2-6-0 similarly displacing the smaller wheeled varieties. Non-standard, and heavy on fuel, they had but a short working life, and the sight seen here, a Caledonian 4-6-0 hauling a rake of twelve-wheeled coaches of West Coast Joint Stock, was, in retrospect, of quite short duration.

PLATE 41

Swedish State Railways
Inside-Cylinder Atlantic No 1024

The Swedes seemed to have more trouble than most in deciding on locomotive cylinder layouts. Above the running plate things were fairly staid, with only a few trade marks such as an enlarged dome casing to contain all possible steam fittings and a well-protected cab (both due to the fierce winters). Below the waistline things got more interesting. Two-, three-, and four-cylinder layouts were common, simple and all kinds of compound (fuel-saving in coal-less Scandinavia was always important), and inside-cylinder designs were greatly favoured because they enabled weight to be saved, even at the price of greater complication of maintenance. Inside-cylinder 'Atlantics' were fairly common elsewhere, but inside-cylinder 2-8-0s were almost unique to Sweden, and common there.

This very neat 4-4-2, built by Nydqvist and Holm in 1908, includes such Swedish exotica as inside cylinders combined with bar frames, and the rather clumsy-looking leading bogie with outside cast frames and uncompensated springing. Piston valves are actuated by inside Walschaerts gear, and the scalloped snow scoops could have been effective only in the shallowest of drifts. Above the running plate the beautifully-clad boiler in planished steel must have dazzled like the snow in winter sunshine. After express work in Sweden had passed mainly to electric traction, these 4-4-2s were rebuilt as 4-6-0s to increase their adhesion and make them more useful on stopping trains.

PLATE 42

North Eastern Railway
Class V1 4-4-2

In 1920, the East coast route between London and Scotland was the 'Atlantic' route, even though the Atlantic Ocean lay on the West side. The reason was, of course, the extensive use of the 4-4-2, or 'Atlantic' type of locomotive by all three partners in the East – the Great Northern, North Eastern, and North British. When the LNER took these over plus the Great Central examples, it thus scooped up most of the 'Atlantics' in Britain. Of the North Eastern engines, there were two main varieties, Worsdell's two-cylinder type as shown, subdivided into the saturated V and superheated V1 classes, and Raven's Z class of three-cylinder engines. The Worsdell Vs were typically Edwardian express power, solid, handsome, and dependable. Reasonably fast and powerful, and moderately efficient, they lasted until the end of the Second World War, after which, still in pre-war green, they were lined up for scrap outside Darlington

shed. The qualities built into these 'Atlantics' were also included in a freight equivalent, the T2 0-8-0, better known as LNER and BR class Q6, which stayed the course to the bitter end when, clanking and wheezing after 40 years of punishment and neglect, they were still the best all-round coal haulers on Tyneside.

PLATE 43

Great Western Railway
'Star' and 'King' class 4-6-0s

First and final generations of Great Western four-cylinder simple designs are shown in this painting. On the left is a slim boilered 'Star', the epoch-making machine which grafted de Glehn's French four-cylinder layout and bogie arrangement on to the basically American two-cylinder engine previously produced by Churchward at Swindon. The result brought new standards of express locomotive performance to Britain's railways, and a number of comparatively feeble attempts were made to emulate this Swindon masterpiece. The North Western, South Western, Great Central, and Lancashire & Yorkshire all built large, four-cylinder, express engines, but failed to appreciate the subleties of Swindon's cylinder, valve, and firebox design. Some 72 'Stars' were built at Swindon, and before his retirement, Churchward had in mind a larger design using the boiler, 6 ft maximum diameter, which he produced for his 4700 class 2-8-0. Collett, his successor, compromised with a smaller boiler and produced the 'Castle' class, and the Churchward big-boilered 4-6-0 finally came out as the 'King' class, seen at the right of the painting.

Massive and regal, the 'Kings' were the largest and most powerful 4-6-0s ever to run in Britain, or for that matter, the whole of Europe. Even in the USA, there were few 4-6-0 classes of comparable dimensions. In their final condition, with larger superheaters and double chimneys, the 'Kings' were capable of producing 2200 indicated horsepower.

PLATE 44

Prussian State Railways
Class S10[1] 4-6-0

The general introduction of superheating in Germany caused compounding to be abandoned, although there continued to be a school of thought averring that superheated compounds were a viable proposition for express work. Thus, all the major State systems persisted with compounds for this duty, and a few were even built for the Reichsbahn in its early, formative, years.

With its vast locomotive fleet, the Prussian State Railway could afford to experiment, and its final express type, the S10 4-6-0, was built in four guises. Two were simple expansion engines, the S10 with four cylinders and the S10[2] with three. In each sub-class, all cylinders drove the leading coupled axle, and the inside valve(s) were conjugated from the outside motion. Class S10[1] covered four-cylinder compounds, of which there were two quite distinct designs. Earliest were the de Glehn engines, with divided drive and staggered cylinders on that classic French arrangement. These had straight-through plate frames. Sharing the bar front and plate rear frames of von Borries design, inherited from earlier 4-4-0 and 4-4-2 engines and shared with the simple expansion designs, were the later compounds as shown. All four cylinders were in line, but the drive was divided between the first and second coupled axles. Evidently there was little to choose between the four types of S10, all were built in significant quantities, and all lasted until just after the Second World War, the two compound versions in Alsace Lorraine, and the simples in Belgium. The bulk, as shown in Reichsbahn colours, disappeared in Germany slightly earlier than these remnants.

PLATE 45

London and South Western Railway
Class T14 4-6-0

Dugald Drummond, after creating some excellent designs in Scotland, took them south to the LSWR and continued production first at Nine Elms and then at Eastleigh. Robustly constructed, and economical to run, the last of his standard, simple designs, continued almost to the end of steam on the Hampshire railways. Strong's was the local ale, and strong were the T9s, M7s, and 700s, but all belonged to an era where successive designs were evolved slowly by adding half an inch here, a ton there, in an almost natural process which could have interested Charles Darwin. However, suddenly, the twentieth century was upon railways, and this seemingly magic figure brought with it a demand for faster and heavier expresses.

Drummond was one of many locomotive men caught unawares, for his beautiful Victorian machines could only to a limited degree be enlarged towards the powers required. To give the man his due, he saw clearly the type of engine that was wanted, but the details were defective. The grate was big enough, but shallow, flat, and difficult to fire. The four cylinders were also ample, but with poor valve and port design, wasteful of steam, they added more to the fireman's burden. Walschaerts valve gear, also new to Drummond, was discreetly hidden behind a gigantic splasher which earned them the sobriquet 'paddleboxes'.

Urie, who succeeded Drummond, fitted some with superheaters and extended smokeboxes as shown, which made the T14s into a reasonable 'second string' engine, but the more hopeless versions were scrapped. Maunsell later defrocked the 'paddleboxes', and gave them lighter, narrower splashers, with a slightly raised running plate, although the dangerous looking bit of valve gear just aft of the cylinders remained exposed. In this final form they roared and thrashed along, on light van trains, or Basingstoke locals, until the last was mercifully put down about 1950.

PLATE 46

Royal and Imperial Austrian State Railways
Class 110 2-6-2

One of the most remarkable locomotive designers the world has ever seen was Austria's Karl Gölsdorf, a sort of Leonardo da Vinci amongst locomotive men. Gölsdorf clearly loved designing, and as his reign extended across the compound and superheater eras, he had ample excuse and opportunity to vary his designs from simple, to two-, three-, and four-cylinder compound, and then to try them all again with superheaters. Appearance, apparently, was a matter of luck, and the end results varied from grotesque to glorious. In the 'glorious' category came most of the express engines, the later 206 and 306 classes of 4-4-0, the 308 'Atlantics', the 10 and 110 2-6-2, as illustrated, and the 210 and 310 2-6-4s. Apart from the 4-4-0s, all the above were four-cylinder compounds, and the 110 class 2-6-2 in this painting was one of the nicest. Any detail taken individually, the tall stovepipe chimney, 'baker's oven'

smokebox doors, driving wheel 'mudguards', hardly sounds pretty, but the overall result is distinctly regal and haughty, and thoroughly befitting the Hapsburgs' royal railway.

At the time of building, the 110s were probably the most powerful express engines in Europe, for they antedated the 'Pacific' type, and were evidently very useful, for the final version survived until the mid 1950s, although by then downgraded to local trains in the Selzthal area.

PLATE 47

Northern Railway of France
4-6-4 No 3.1102

Early in the twentieth century, in 1911, while most of the world was just beginning to turn from four-coupled express power to 4-6-0s and 4-6-2s, the CF du Nord jumped a stage and built the world's first 4-6-4 tender engines, antedating the New York Central's 'Hudsons' by nearly 20 years. Exactly what inspired the construction of such huge engines when the famous de Glehn 'Atlantics' were doing such good work, is now somewhat of a mystery, for the later and much smaller 'Pacifics' were able to handle all the fastest and heaviest expresses until de Caso reintroduced the 4-6-4 type just prior to the Nord's absorption into the SNCF.

Whatever the reasons behind their construction, the two engines were a substantial step forward in size and power over anything else in Europe. Apart from this, they also included physical features of an unusual and experimental nature. The unusual, indeed unique, feature was a direct result of their size. Being straightforward de Glehn compounds, they had low-pressure cylinders between the frames, driving the leading coupled axle, and the problem arose as to how they could be squeezed in. The usual side-by-side layout was too cramped and restricted the bearing areas, so the two cylinders were staggered, one ahead of the other, the front one having a long piston rod passing close by the wall of the other cylinder. It was all very clever, as an exercise in locomotive architecture; but attending to the gland of the front, or changing piston rings on the rear cylinder must have challenged the skill of even the best French fitters!

The other feature, on No 3.1102 only (as painted by Le Fleming), was the provision of a water-tube firebox, also tried out on 4-4-4 No 2.741, probably as a result of Herr Brotan's work in Austria—Hungary. No 3.1102, later fitted with a normal Belpaire firebox, was ultimately sectionalised for exhibition, and was last reported amongst preserved locomotives stored at Chalons-sur-Saone.

PLATE 48

Great Northern Railway
Class O1 2-8-0

Before developing such enthusiasm for three-cylinder types, Gresley produced two very sound and up-to-date two-cylinder designs, the K1 and K2, small- and large-boilered mixed traffic 2-6-0s, also these heavy freight and mineral 2-8-0s. Indeed, had it not been for the difficulties caused by the First World War, there might have been a passenger version as well. It was one of these O1s which formed the basis for Gresley's first three-cylinder design; No 461, part of a batch in hand, was built as an experiment, with all three cylinders driving the second coupled axle, and the centre valve actuated by the same arrangement of floating rocking shafts as had first appeared on a Berlin suburban tank design a year earlier.

In trying out three-cylinder propulsion, Gresley was in friendly territory, for his nearest neighbours, the North Eastern, Great Central, and Great Eastern, had all tried out the system, although only the North Eastern used them at all extensively. By using the O1 as a base design, Gresley was able to carry out tests between two locomotive classes differing only in the number of cylinders used, and the results were sufficiently good to convince him that three cylinders were the answer to nearly everything; only a few smaller, inside-cylinder designs subsequently appearing with less.

In service, the O1s lasted well into BR days, although latterly they had been reclassified O3 as Thompson wanted all the 'ones' for his own designs. At the end, the O3s were to be found mostly in the Doncaster-Scunthorpe area, on heavy mineral traffic, working from Frodingham shed.

PLATE 49

Italian State Railways
Class 745 2-8-0

In the early years of the century, when the State Railways had been formed to take over the various struggling and impecunious company systems, Italian trackwork was of a decidedly light and rickety character. So indeed, were the locomotives, and substantial numbers of larger, more powerful, and almost modern engines were put into service, as replacements.

Building locomotives is, however, a quicker and cheaper process than track renewal, and the new types had consequently to be built down to severe restrictions of both axle loadings and total weight. Despite this, railways in Italy offered no easy operational task, due to the generally mountainous terrain, and multi-wheeled engines became necessary – indeed, Europe's first 4-8-0 was built for Italy.

Amongst the locomotives inherited by the State Railways was a useful class of inside-cylinder 2-6-0, and these were multiplied and modified until four basic varieties existed – compound or simple, each with large or small driving wheels. When a larger, but lightweight, passenger design was needed, the basic 'Mogul' was extended to a 2-8-0, and a large, wide firebox, boiler applied. The use of inside instead of outside cylinders saved a substantial amount of weight at the front end, at the expense of heavy bearing pressures and consequent maintenance expenses. An unusual feature, as with the 2-6-0s, was the placing of steam chests and valves, together with the valve gear, outside, thus reducing the amount of machinery positioned inaccessibly between the frames.

The leading truck was of the 'Zara' type, with the rear end mounted on the leading coupled axle, which had side play. With weight and side control taken through a central pivot, the arrangement acted almost as well as a four-wheel bogie in traversing curves, and was later adopted by no less an engineer than Chapelon, for his 141P class of 2-8-2.

PLATE 50

Central Railroad of New Jersey
'Camelback' 4-8-0

The Wootten firebox, extending to the full width allowed by the loading gauge, was evolved in America to give a maximum size grate area suitable for burning anthracite. At about the same time as Wootten introduced his firebox, Belpaire in Belgium was also working on locomotives with oversize grate areas, presumably for consuming low grade fuel (see plate 25).

In America it was thought at the time that the driver would be unable to see past the great firebox ahead of him, and the 'Camelback' engine was evolved, or rather exhumed from Ross Winans' experiments of the 1840s with the driver closeted in his own private cab astride the boiler, for all the world like a mahout in charge of an elephant, but taking advantage of the Sultan's absence by sitting in the howdah! The fireman was left in his usual place behind the firebox backplate, with a vestigial shelter to guard him from the elements. Why the engineer needed such palatial accommodation has never been satisfactorily explained—he could only occupy one side at a time, and a one-sided cab, rather like a London bus, would appear adequate, and would thus allow more cash to be devoted to improving the fireman's quarters. However, this was not to be, and after this outrageously unconventional cab had been designed, conservatism took over and blocked any attempt at improvement.

In the end most railroads did away with centre-cab engines, mainly on the grounds of safety—the driver could die at the throttle and the fireman know nothing of it; but here and there 'Camelbacks' survived almost to the end of steam. One such line was the CRRNJ which, in addition to owning 4-8-0 freight engines as shown here, hauled New York commuters with camelback 4-6-0s for some years after the Second World War, these being just about the last of the type in main-line service anywhere. The 'Camelback' never prospered abroad because outside the USA it usually ran into difficulties with the loading gauge.

PLATE 51

Bavarian State Railways
Class G4/5H 2-8-0

Whilst Maffei's Munich works were gaining fame as builders of elegant and efficient express locomotives, the same design features of bar frames and four-cylinder compound propulsion were being built into two series of freight engines for the Bavarian State Railways. For general freight work, the 2-8-0 shown here was built in large numbers; and for the heaviest mountain duties, an 0-10-0 was produced, of similar size, features, and appearance, but having all its weight available for adhesion. Ninety of the ten-coupled type were placed in service, and substantially more of the 'Consolidation' class shown were built. Compared with the contemporary passenger engines, these had shorter lives, being replaced by the simpler Prussian and German standard classes which, with two or three cylinders, and no compound complications, were a better proposition as far as maintenance went, and equally efficient. Apart from some 2-8-0s for the Baden State, and Swiss Gotthard railways, the Maffei freight designs were not exported like the passenger versions, and none have been in existence for many years now.

PLATE 52

Great Central Railway
'Director' Class 4-4-0

Named after directors of the GCR these Robinson-designed 4-4-0s were undoubtedly the finest express engines owned by the GC. Compared with the larger 4-4-2 and 4-6-0 types, the 'Directors' had an equal grate area, better cylinder design, and less restricted air intake around the ashpan, and could consequently steam harder for longer periods than their impressive looking but internally-congested sisters. Moreover, the 'Directors' were handsome-looking engines, especially after the inheriting LNER had removed the coupling rod skirting, exposing the delightful curves of the running plate valance, and revealing rather more of the driving wheels than was considered decent in Victorian days.

A later series of 'Directors' was built after the First World War, and some of these were given foreign names such as *Mons*, to commemorate battles which indirectly, and as a remote consequence led to the end of Britain's colourful and prosperous, if not particularly imaginative, 'pre-grouping' railway era. However, the 'Directors' were splendid engines. Nigel Gresley, the LNER's new Chief Mechanical Engineer, was a big enough man to see the worth of another's designs, and 25 more 'Directors', more in fact than the GC ever owned, were built under Gresley for use in Scotland. This final batch, possibly to hide their Sassenach origins, were given names as Scottish as oatcakes and haggis, like 'Luckie Mucklebackit,' and 'Bailie MacWheeble', were rarely seen south of the Tweed, and probably never touched buffers with the original Gorton products.

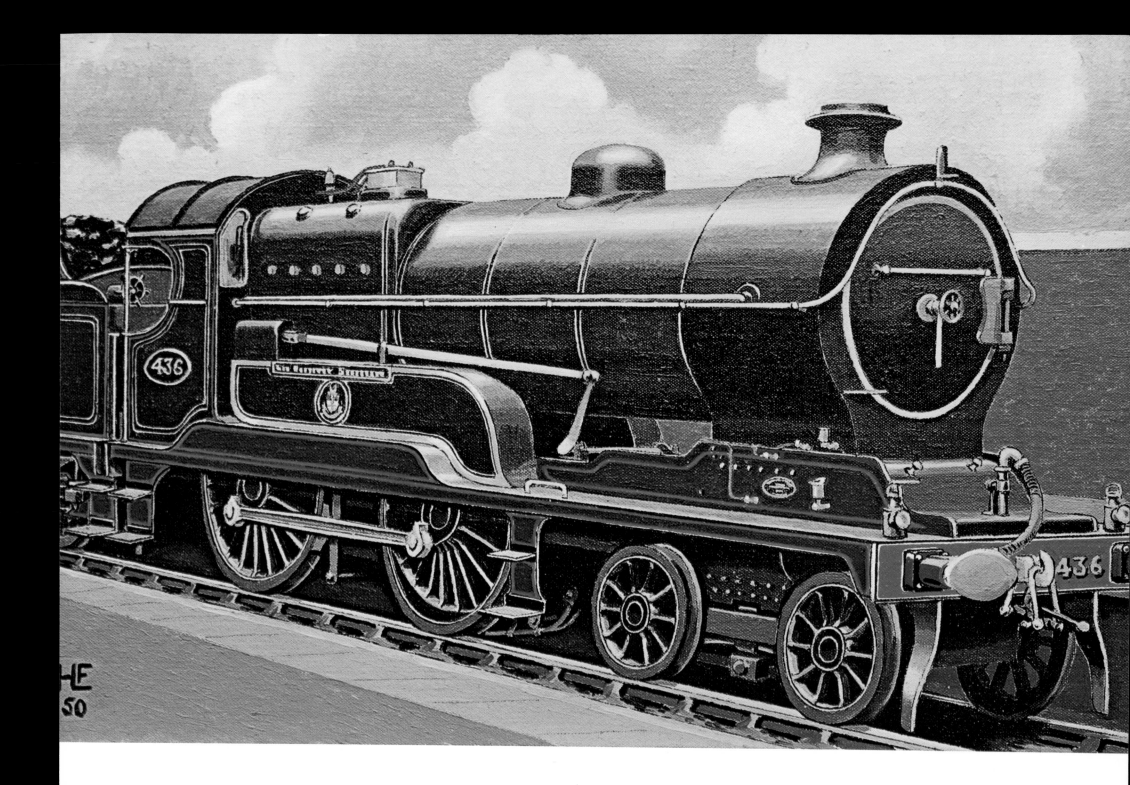

PLATE 53

Portuguese Railways
1501 Class 4-6-2

Heavy trains were never a feature of the railways in Portugal, and despite the severe gradients encountered, there was thus little need for locomotives of high power. The 4-6-0 was the most popular passenger type, and came in a number of different varieties—assorted four-cylinder compounds, and two-cylinder simples with inside or with outside cylinders. The only 'Pacifics' were two batches of almost identical Henschel four-cylinder superheated compounds, one of which is illustrated here.

Despite its German build, the engine is of thoroughly French style technically, (like many others in Portugal) having the de Glehn cylinder layout, plate frames, a thoroughly Gallic leading bogie, and that French speciality, a Belpaire firebox with trapezoidal grate, ie narrow at the front and wide at the rear.

For most of their lives, these 'Pacifics' have been centred on the southern lines working into Lisbon, but right at the end of broad-gauge steam in Portugal, a few have been transferred to the north, for the routes serving Oporto and the Douro valley.

PLATE 54

Swedish State Railways
Class 4-6-2

Sweden was not, in later years, one of the European countries prominent in the advance of steam locomotive technology, despite the considerable national engineering tradition, because after the 1920s electric traction was rapidly extended on main lines throughout the country. Steam development thus, by and large, ended in the era of the 4-6-0s and 2-8-0s. That of Switzerland followed a similar pattern. Each country produced one class of steam locomotive which could, by European standards, be classed 'big', but whereas Switzerland's was a 2-10-0 freighter for the Gotthard main line, Sweden's was this handsome four-cylinder compound Pacific, for express passenger work, introduced in 1913, and a very creditable product for its date. Before they had paid for themselves, these 4-6-2s were largely displaced by new electrics, though some continued to work into the 1950s. Fortunately a purchaser was found in neighbouring Denmark, who ran them as their class 'E'. The Danes indeed liked them so much that nearly 40 years later they built some more themselves! These later examples had improved front ends with double chimneys. Examples of both early and late machines were still to be found on the Danish lines in 1970.

Strange to say, the Swedes eventually decided that they wanted one of their largest steam engines for their railway museum, and one was repurchased from Denmark for this purpose.

PLATE 55

Baden State Railways
Class IVh 4-6-2

J. A. Maffei of Munich, Bavaria, were renowned in the early twentieth century for designing and building the most elegant of locomotives, combining the European four-cylinder compound system of propulsion with American pattern bar frames. Most of these were for the native Bavarian State Railways, and its associate, the Pfälzbahn (Palatinate Railway), but numerous other administrations were attracted to, and purchased, the designs. Of the express types, there were 4-4-2 and 4-6-0 classes with narrow fireboxes, and wide firebox designs with the 4-4-2, 4-4-4, 2-6-2 and 4-6-2 arrangements. The 4-4-4 was a solitary high-speed engine having 2 200 mm (7 ft $2\frac{1}{2}$ in) driving wheels, and is now in Nuremberg Museum, after a career which included speeding just below the 100 mph mark. The 2-6-2 type was built only for the Baden State Railway, which also bought a smaller 'Pacific', class IVg, and the

4-6-2 class depicted here, which were the largest of the Maffei express designs. With 2 100 mm (6 ft $10\frac{1}{2}$ in) diameter drivers, only a little smaller than the 4-4-4, these were employed on the fastest expresses along the Rhine valley, to and from Basel. Mechanically, they were unique in presenting a new solution to the problem of fitting large-diameter cylinders between the frames. As may be clearly seen, the two inside cylinders are inclined at different angles and 'wrapped round' each other, so enabling the crank centres to be set closer. Thus, there was no need to 'dish' the driving wheels, to allow room for large outside low-pressure cylinders. Upon the formation of the Deutsche Reichsbahn, they became class 18[3], and were retained for special high-speed duties until the mid-1960s, two in West Germany at the Minden testing station, and the third, rebuilt after the war with a welded boiler, for similar duties at Halle.

PLATE 56

Bavarian State Railways
Shed scene

Bavarian locomotives, as designed and built at J. A. Maffei's works, in Munich, had a far more elegant and less starkly utilitarian appearance than those of the northern Prussian plains. Presumably this was to be expected from a country where men wore green flashes and feathers in their hats, and went on a gigantic beer drinking spree every October! Bavarian engines were none the less individualistic for leaning more towards Vienna than Berlin. Maffei first introduced modern, American type, bar frames into European practice, and among other achievements, built the largest Mallet locomotives in Europe, some huge 0-8-8-0T bankers. Seen in the foreground of this painting is the front of a Maffei 'Pacific', of the S3/6 class so justly famous in the locomotive world. The row of cylinder and valve covers exposed to view beneath the conical smokebox door was a striking sight when first encountered,

perhaps at the buffers' end at Frankfurt station. Above the outside (low pressure) cylinder may be distinguished the supremely simple starting arrangements of the Maffei compounds. The two little valves, for admitting high-pressure steam to the low-pressure steam chests, are controlled directly from the reversing quadrant. In full forward or back gear, the valves open, but as soon as cut-off is reduced below a predetermined figure, the valves close and full compound working is commenced.
In the background is one of the light 2-6-0s, class G3/4H, a simple superheated engine for secondary services on both main lines and branches.

PLATE 57

Saxon State Railways
Class X1h 4-6-2

Three-cylinder propulsion gained immense impetus in Germany during the First World War, and from that time onwards, Germany has been the world leader in three-cylinder loco-motives. A modest start was made with a three-cylinder 2-6-2T for the Berlin suburban services, in 1902, and in 1913 a larger 2-8-2T was built for the same purpose as the Great Eastern 'Decapod', to equal with steam an electric's acceleration. This larger engine made history by being the world's first three-cylinder design to use conjugated valve gear, whereby the motion for the inside valve was derived from that of the two outside gears. A system of horizontal shafts and vertical levers achieved this motion, the same as was tried by Gresley the following year on his 2-8-0 No 461. The Prussian State Railways took to the system with some enthusiasm, and during the war built large numbers of 2-10-0s, class G12, not only for themselves, but

also as a German standard heavy freight engine, supplied to other State lines as well. Amongst these was the Saxon State Railways which, in 1917, adopted the system themselves, and applied it to a group of 4-6-2 express engines, as shown. These 15 locomotives thus antedated Gresley's conjugate-gear 'Pacifics' by five years, but were not multiplied, although lasting long, as German class 18°, and working into the 1960s, still in their home territory but now within East Germany.

PLATE 58

Prussian State Railways
Class T14^1 2-8-2T

One of the very useful, all-purpose tank engines of the Prussian system, is shown here in its later guise as a German State Railways class 93$^{5-12}$, in the all embracing, Teutonic numbering system adopted by Reichsbahn. Only the tank and bunker design differed from the earlier and neater T14 class, and the engine shown here was thoroughly up to date, as were indeed most of the engines built for Prussia in the twentieth century. Superheaters and long lap piston valves gave these 2-8-2Ts a snappy performance, and although classed officially as freight engines, they performed a good deal of heavy suburban work, especially around Berlin, Frankfurt and Hamburg. What is more, they were sufficiently lightly loaded on each axle to be permitted on branch lines, and like most of the Prussian designs, they spread widely into other areas of Germany after the formation of the Reichsbahn. It is worth mentioning here the two other tank designs which complemented the T14s. There was the T16 group of 0-10-0Ts using the same-sized cylinders and wheels as the T14, but with smaller boiler. With lower horsepower, but greater adhesion weight, these were designed as heavy shunters, and banking engines, and even today may be found on passenger work over 1 in 17 gradients in southern Germany. Purely as a passenger engine, there is also the T18 4-6-4T, and the three designs made an excellently-proportioned trio for short-distance workings, two of which are still active in the 1970s.

PLATE 59

New York Central Railroad
Class CC1s 0-8-8-0

Most 'Mallets' in America, and for that
matter elsewhere, were designed and
built for road work, whether this was
main- or branch-line haulage, or banking.
For the heaviest duties in hump and
other large shunting yards handling
weighty traffic, a number of American
lines operated giant 0-8-8-0 compound
'Mallets', of which this NYC engine is a
good example. Eclipsing all other
shunting engines in size and power,
nothing to equal their brute capacity has
been built since for shunting duties.
Having said that, there is little more to
relate. No technical features of particular
interest were included, and the design
was simply a standard 2-8-8-0 Mallet,
shorn of its leading pony truck, and
built with slightly smaller wheels than
were used in road service. These heavy
shifters lasted through the Second World
War, and were scrapped during the age
of frantic dieselisation which followed.

PLATE 60

Virginian Railway

2-10-10-2

This vivid painting depicts two of America's most remarkable 'Mallets' working on their designed duty, that of banking coal trains over the Allegheny mountain range. Perhaps even more remarkable is the fact that no photographs seem to exist of them on this duty, so that the Le Fleming painting is a valuable and unique pictorial representation of this impressive, and doubtless ear-shattering, operation.

Compound 'Mallets' were early introduced by the Virginian for the 14-mile climb from Elsmore to Clark's Gap, of which the final 11 miles climbed solidly at 1 in 50, broken only where compensated for curvature, some of which was of 485 ft radius. To add to the operating difficulties, there were also five tunnels. With train loads rapidly increasing in the boom years of the early twentieth century, the 'Mallets' quickly grew in size and power, and due to the peculiar circumstances of the railway, banking engines progressed to train engines instead of the usual reverse retrogression. Thus the 2-6-6-0s built to bank 2-8-0 hauled trains, became train engines, with banking duties taken over by larger 2-8-8-2s. A trio of 'Triplex' six-cylinder 2-8-8-8-4 compounds, with driving wheels under the tender, were tried unsuccessfully and the final steam power to conquer Clark's Gap were these stupendous Alco 2-10-10-2s. Used in pairs to bank 6 000-ton trains hauled by a 2-8-8-2, these ten-coupled 'Mallets' boasted the largest diameter cylinders (48-in LP), and the largest diameter boilers (9ft $10\frac{1}{2}$ in), ever applied to a locomotive. From these dimensions was produced 147 000 lb of tractive effort, working compound. Even with America's generous loading gauge, the locomotives had to have cabs and cylinders removed for transit during delivery.

PLATE 61

Pennsylvania Railroad
Class A5s 0-4-0

An engine without a tender was
anathema to most American engineers,
and even when they wanted a short
wheelbase 0-4-0 for pottering about the
sharp curves of dock and warehouse
areas, they usually hung a tender on
behind—and a bogie tender at that.
Thus, we have here a locomotive with
twice as many wheels on the tender as on
the engine! Despite its humble duties,
the A5s was a modern and powerful
little engine, with superheater, piston
valves, and, as can be clearly seen, a wide,
Belpaire firebox. Weighing some 60
long tons, and with a tractive effort just
over 30 000 lb, she was a more powerful
freight engine than most pre-grouping
British railways possessed. The PRR
owned a complete range of shunting
engines, largely standardised in design,
from these little four-wheelers, through
0-6-0 and 0-8-0 types, to vast 0-8-8-0
compound 'Mallets' for the heaviest
humping duties.

PLATE 62

Great Eastern Railway
Class D81 0-6-0

These, the last and largest of the Great Eastern freight fleet, were for many years the largest 0-6-0s in Britain, or for that matter, outside the USA. Better known as the LNER J20 class, they incorporated in their design the same boiler as was used for Holden's 1500 class 4-6-0, later LNER B12. With nearly 30 000 lb of tractive effort, they were among the most powerful freight engines in Britain when built, and were only substantially exceeded by the Lancashire & Yorkshire, and the North Eastern, 0-8-0s, and the Great Northern, Great Western, and Somerset & Dorset 2-8-0s.

The reason behind such a large engine on the Great Eastern, where the suburban and the rural traffic were the dominant features, was the heavy domestic coal traffic between Whitemoor yard, near March, and London. The main line of the rival Great Northern was really too full of fast passenger and freight trains to pay much more than lip service to the competition for the north-east London coal trade, and the Great Eastern, with its easier route, took the lion's share. Largely replaced in later years by 'Austerity' 2-8-0s, the last J20s managed to survive until the early 1960s, and the beginnings of dieselisation. They remained the champion British 0-6-0s for a whole generation, and were just, but only just, eclipsed by Bulleid's Southern Railway Q1 class, during the Second World War.

PLATE 63

Lancashire and Yorkshire Railway
Hughes 0-8-0

With its great, fat, boiler, perched up on a short wheelbase, it is difficult to view a 'Lanky' large 0-8-0 without drawing an immediate parallel to a circus elephant standing on a tub! For all this, they were powerful and impressive engines, and amongst the ranks of British 0-8-os exceeded only by Raven's North Eastern monsters with three cylinders. Derived directly from Aspinall's smaller-boilered version, some of the Hughes engines were built new, and others rebuilt from Aspinall engines. With the small-boiler survivors, the whole group eventually numbered nearly 300 engines, and were the mainstay of the Lancashire & Yorkshire's arduous mineral traffic, characterised not only by the weighty loadings, but by the severe gradients of the trans-Pennine routes. Despite their power, they were mostly replaced, at a fairly rapid rate, after absorption into the LMS, by a new Fowler design of less power and considerably less adequate bearing dimensions. Some Hughes 0-8-os remained at work in 1939, and therefore 1945. After the Second World War, the Fowler 0-8-os quickly followed the last of their 'Lanky' forerunners to the scrapheap.

PLATE 64

Norwegian State Railways
Class 31D 4-8-0

Norwegian and Swedish locomotives had a number of things in common, including a neat, clean appearance, typified in this compound 4-8-0. They were, of course, neighbours, but in the world of locomotive design, this did not count for much, as we all know. Apart from the handful of 'Dovregubben' 2-8-4s, various 4-8-0 classes were the backbone of Norwegian power until electrification, combining, as they did, a reasonably high power output on a low axle-load.

Train weights were moderate, allowing these smallish engines to cope on the severe gradients through the Nordic Alps, although double heading was certainly practised regularly. Norway was, one feels, ideal Garratt country, and such an articulated blasting through the rugged terrain shown here, its unsynchronised exhaust echoing and re-echoing from the rocky mountain sides, would have been a sight and sound sufficient to impress even the riders of the Valkyrie!

Norwegian 4-8-0s were all four-cylinder machines, and mainly compounds, although a few were simple-expansion engines. During the German occupation of the Second World War, numerous Prussian G10 0-10-0 and wartime 52 class 2-10-0s were drafted into Norway to haul the military traffic, and the latter were found to be so useful that in the declining days of post-war steam, they displaced many of the indigenous 4-8-0 type, a few of which have nevertheless managed to last right to the end, in 1971.

PLATE 65

Austrian Federal Railways
Class 113 4-8-0

In 1915 the Südbahn, or Austrian Southern Railway, built two large 4-8-0 passenger engines for the principal expresses over the famous Semmering Pass, between Gloggnitz and Mürzzuschlag, where 1 in 40 ruling gradients prevailed. Five more of the same type were built for the Kaschau Oderberger Railway, connecting Austria and Hungary through the Tatra mountain district, and when the Austrian railways were reorganised after the loss of the old Hapsburg empire, this Südbahn design was taken as a basis for the first new main-line passenger power.

The principal changes were in the cylinders, the new 113 class having poppet instead of piston valves, these being of the Lentz type actuated by Walschaerts motion. The cylinders were also altered in proportions, being of smaller diameter and longer stroke than the original design. Forty of these excellent engines were built between 1924 and 1927, and were the mainstay of express services on the southern main line; they also worked the western line, particularly before the arrival of the larger 2-8-4s.

During the German occupation of Austria they became class 33[1], and in this guise have been well known to visitors to Austria in post-war years. No. 33.107 was the first main line tender engine fitted with the Giesl ejector, in 1951, and so successful did this prove to be that all the remainder of the class in Austria were so fitted. The sight and sound of one of these, hauling 17 coaches over the Semmering, piloted and banked by a 2-10-2T, was one of the great experiences of the steam age.

PLATE 66

Danish State Railways
Class H 2-8-0

Denmark, being a generally flat and level country, with little in the way of heavy industry, had small need for large numbers of powerful freight locomotives. Indeed, it is surprising that anything so big as the H class was considered necessary at all. Larger than any British 2-8-0, other than the Great Western 4700 class, the Danish locomotives had three-cylinder propulsion, all connecting rods driving on the second coupled axle. Individual Walschaerts gear was used to actuate each valve, and the primary motion for these was derived from return cranks mounted on the crankpins of the third coupled axle. On the left-hand side, there was a double return-crank, the outer member of which drove the expansion link for the inside motion, by means of a rocking shaft. This arrangement is shown clearly in the painting.

A feature of Danish locomotives was the display of national colours on a band round the chimney; State railways with white sandwiched between red, as shown, and private railways with the colours reversed. Despite the virtual disappearance of steam from the Danish railways, one of the H class was still operable in September 1970, when it participated in a steam tour for British enthusiasts.

PLATE 67

Lübeck Büchener Eisenbahn

2-8-0

Among the larger and more important of Germany's private railways was the Lübeck Büchener. This would not have been so had it remained a line running simply between the two towns included in its title, but it also operated an important main line from Lübeck to Hamburg. For this line, engines of a main-line character were used, and the express engines included a lighter version of the Prussian State Railways S10^2 three-cylinder 4-6-0. Between the wars, the railway invested in some new power of modern design; and this included such exotic items as streamlined 2-4-2Ts for working double-decker push-and-pull 'inter-city' trains.

Freight traffic was important, too, and for this were built the batch of 2-8-0s, one of which is depicted here. Only eight were built, to meet the needs of a smallish private railway, and when the system was eventually incorporated into the Reichsbahn, at the outbreak of the Second World War, these engines became Nos 56 3001 to 56 3008. Although built generally to German standards, they were as a class, non-standard, and with plenty of the ubiquitous 2-10-0s available after the war, they were scrapped or sold. At least one went to the Öst Hannoversche Eisenbahn, and another was recently discovered working on a coal-mining railway near Aachen, on the Belgian border.

PLATE 68

London and North Eastern Railway
Class A1 4-6-2

Accelerating through the suburbs of North London, with a train of teak finished stock, is one of Gresley's original 'Pacifics', the first 'big engines' to be built in quantity for a British railway. Gresley clearly saw the rightness of building engines big enough to cope without assistance, and in his time, and after, double-heading was a rare sight on the East coast line. How different this was from his western competitors, who never really grew out of the habit of double-heading.

In their original form, Gresley's engines lacked the long-lap, long-travel valves of modern practice, but this was remedied after trials between his 4-6-2s and Great Western 'Castles', which proved in the 1925 Exchange trials capable of giving a snappier and more economical performance. The resulting improved 'Pacifics' were soon making impressive feats of speed and haulage, and an authenticated 108 mph was attained with one of this breed, appropriately named after racehorses, although to non-racegoers some of these names must have sounded strange. However, to a railway which served Newmarket and had its 'plant' at Doncaster, all was logic. The A1 led to the A3, and later to the A4, with its authenticated world speed record. The Achilles heel of these designs was Gresley's derived motion for the inside valve. With the valve set *when hot*, to eliminate expansion errors, and with first-class maintenance, the gear was fine, but in wartime and post-war years, the characteristically irregular beat was an all too frequent symptom of a Gresley engine pulling hard.

Thompson tried out a gawky, modified design, but Peppercorn's final variation on the Gresley 'Pacific' theme, with independent valve gear, larger grate, and roller bearings, was a contender for the title of Britain's finest express engine.

PLATE 69

German Group
Heavy three-cylinder power

The development of German three-cylinder power is outlined under caption, No 57. Representative of the machines built for the heaviest mountain duties are the three illustrated. On the left is 2-8-2 No 39.117, a Prussian design, class P10, for heavy passenger work. Significant is the fact that conjugated valve gear was abandoned on these machines, never to be reinstated. So useful did these engines prove that they were made in quantity by the Reichsbahn until 250 were in service. An interesting mechanical feature was that primary motion for the inside valve was taken from a double return-crank on the left-hand side, all valve gear being driven from the third coupled axle, although the cylinders drove the second. The decidedly French firebox included a Belpaire flat top, and 'trapezoidal' grate.

Next to the '39' is one of Germany's workhorses, the 44 class 2-10-0 which, built to a 20-ton axle load, has been in the front rank of European freight power from 1925 until the present day. The starting tractive effort of 64000 lb at 85 per cent boiler pressure may seem high for the adhesion weight, but in practice they are exceptionally sure-footed and handle immense mineral trains with little apparent effort. Furthermore, they are permitted to run at 50 mph, which they achieve freely, and may thus be used to advantage on heavy, mountain, passenger trains.

The third locomotive shown, the 84 class 2-10-2T, was specially designed for passenger service on the steeply graded Heidenau—Altenburg branch into the Harz mountains in Saxony. Slightly lighter than the previous 85 class which hauled passenger trains up the 1 in 18 gradients of the Höllental line in the Black Forest, the 84s' route had been converted from narrow gauge, and to allow this vast locomotive to traverse the resulting sharp curves, Schwartzkopf–Eckhardt bogies were fitted to each end. Nos 84 003 and 004 were two-cylinder engines, the outer axles being gear-coupled on the Lüttermöller system, but 84 007 shown here is a three-cylinder locomotive.

PLATE 70

German State Railways
Class 80 0-6-0T

The standard designs evolved for the Reichsbahn between 1925 and 1940 were undoubtedly the most complete unified range the world has ever seen. All bore an unmistakable family likeness and, apart from the usual main-line engines included in other standardisation schemes, there were shunting, and even narrow-gauge designs.

As things turned out, some of the 'standards' were built in such small quantities that they never approached the totals of the engines they were intended to replace, which latter often outlasted the newer standards. In this category come the standard, or *einheits* shunting engines, of which there were four classes, light and heavy 0-6-0T, an 0-8-0T and an 0-10-0T, classes 89, 80, 81, and 87 respectively. Shown here is the 80 class, a chunky 0-6-0T with 18-ton axle load, the most numerous built, although they only numbered 40. Although so small, all modern features were built into these locomotives, superheaters, piston valves, and modern cylinder design. In post-war days, diesel shunters have made heavy inroads into their duties, although one or two are believed to be still at work in and around East Berlin.

PLATE 71

Eastern Railway of France
Series 13 4-8-2

The Est, or Eastern Railway had a point in common with England's Great Western, in that express engines with wide fireboxes and trailing trucks were not generally favoured – whilst the other lines were introducing 'Atlantics', the Est was building France's largest 4-4-0s, and similarly, when the others progressed to 'Pacifics', the Est turned to large 4-6-0s. The exception was the design shown, probably completed only after a great deal of thinking in terms of the rival 4-8-0 type.

Completed concurrently with 4-8-2 express designs for the Paris, Lyon and Mediterranean Railway, and the Northern of Spain, the Est design was undoubtedly the best-looking of the trio, and one of the most handsome 4-8-2 designs Europe has ever seen. Mechanically, a pure-bred de Glehn compound with divided drive and low-pressure cylinders inside, a severe design problem existed in how to fit the large low-pressure cylinders between the frames and, more important, how to find room for adequate bearings. The driving wheels were dished outwards, enabling the axleboxes to be spread as widely as possible, but even then, there was insufficient room between the leading coupled axleboxes to spread the crank centres enough to accommodate the cylinders. The answer decided upon was unique in its ingenuity – the crossheads were designed such that the connecting rod was offset about two inches from the piston rod centre! In practice this worked well enough, although an official speed limit of 100 kph indicated some apprehension about side-thrusts which could occur. Altogether, 91 of the design were built for the Est, and also the Etat (State) railways, the latter gradually migrating to the Est in later years. After the formation of the SNCF, or French National Railways, these became class 241A, and most were eventually fitted with multiple-jet chimneys, feed-water heaters, and larger smoke-deflectors, all of which improved their appearance yet further. They were still to be seen on major express trains in the early 1960s.

PLATE 72

Great Northern Railway (USA
Class R1 4-8-4

One of the most popular steam types in the last days of steam in North America was the 4-8-4. A splendid 'all rounder', the 4-8-4 was equally at ease in freight or express passenger work, was able to develop well over 6 000 hp, and to run almost 30 000 miles a month. Railroads in the west soon adopted the type for heavy express work, after the Northern Pacific pioneered the type in 1927, and among the early users was the Great Northern.

These engines were unusual amongst American 4-8-4s, firstly in having Belpaire fireboxes, the only 4-8-4s in the world so fitted, so far as the writer is aware. Additionally, they were painted in the GN's pleasant green livery, as a change from the almost universal black of American steam power.

Strictly mountain engines, the R1s were subsequently joined by the later R2 class, the latter having round-top fireboxes, and 6 ft 8 in wheels for high-speed express work over easier sections. It always seems strange that whereas England's Great Northern never went in for the Belpaire firebox, its namesake across the Atlantic was one of the very few US railroads to make extensive use of it.

PLATE 73

Union Pacific Railroad
9000 Class 4-12-2

The immense locomotive seen in this painting was one of the most remarkable steam types ever built. They were the largest three-cylinder engines in the world, the largest twelve-coupled type, and, with the exception of the solitary Russian experimental 4-14-4, they had the longest rigid-coupled wheelbase ever applied to a locomotive. All these giant dimensions, remarkable even in the American world of massive locomotives, were achieved by steady progress towards the bold design which, as far back as 1926, reached limits never to be surpassed.

From the standard Harriman Lines 2-10-2, a three-cylinder 4-10-2 was developed; and finally the American Locomotive company, in conjunction with Union Pacific design staff, built the first of the 9000s. Driving wheels were 5 ft 7 in diameter, a remarkable size for ten-coupled power, let alone twelve-coupled. To accommodate

wheels of this size, the fixed wheelbase was 30 ft 8 in. The drive was divided, outside cylinders connecting with the third coupled axle, whilst the inside cylinder drove the second, cranked, axle. British engineers, particularly former LNER men, will be interested to learn that the centre valve was actuated by Gresley's '2 to 1' motion, clearly depicted in the painting.

Apparently the Gresley conjugated valve gear gave some trouble in service, and on a few locos, it was replaced by a third set of Walschaerts gear, although the improvement was insufficient to warrant further conversions. The 4-12-2s lasted well into the diesel era, and the last was withdrawn early in 1956, only a short time before steam operation on the Union Pacific ceased altogether.

PLATE 74

Northern Pacific Railway
Class Z8 2-8-8-4

These locomotives were, at the time of building, the largest in the world, and in some respects, remain serious contenders for that title. With so many variables, it is difficult to balance claims made on various bases such as overall weight, tractive effort, adhesion weight, grate area, and tested hp. The Union Pacific 'Big Boy' 4-8-8-4 excels in the matter of total engine weight, and with its magnificent appearance, strong publicity, and accessibility for viewing, has been generally accepted as the world's largest.

However, the Northern Pacific engines here depicted exceed the 'Big Boys' in grate area, adhesion weight, and tractive effort, even though first built so long ago as 1928. Their *raison d'être* was the haulage of 4 000-ton trains between Glendive, Montana and Mandan, North Dakota, over sections including gradients of 1 in 91. Locally mined 'Rosebud' sub-bituminous coal, of only 10 000 BThU lb (when dried) was used as fuel, and to burn this, an immense firebox with a grate area of 182 square feet was included in the design. This is equivalent to a grate of about 120 square feet designed to burn Welsh steam coal, and the potential ihp of the engine was about 7 500. Located as they were amongst the 'badlands' of the northern US, passing through the Yellowstone National Park, these were the first 2-8-8-4 type built, and indeed, the first 'Mallets' with a four-wheeled trailing truck beneath the firebox; their scene of activities gave the name 'Yellowstone' to the type.

PLATE 75

Denver and Rio Grande Western Railroad
1600 class 4-8-2

Today, the title of this Company brings to many people's minds only the surviving steam-powered three-foot gauge line from Durango to Silverton, still owned by them. The original Denver and Rio Grande was indeed exclusively narrow-gauge, and as such at one time stretched from Denver to Salt Lake City. But this was no use as a link in a transcontinental route, and from the 1890s onwards the original narrow-gauge system was either converted or by-passed with new routes, leaving only a few short sections.

It was not until the 1930s, however, that the Rio Grande really obtained a competitive position in the long-haul market, when it acquired the Denver and Salt Lake line with its newly-opened short cut through the Moffatt tunnel. To work the passenger services on this mountainous main line through the centre of the Colorado Rockies, Baldwin built these heavy three-cylinder 4-8-2s just before the Depression. They were the only American three-cylinder locomotives to be used extensively for passenger duties over a long period, and some of their success must be due to their use of independent Walchaerts gear for each cylinder, rather than the Gresley gear used on most American three-cylinder locomotives. The 1600s survived the Second World War, but were then overwhelmed by the flood of diesels which swept throughout the land.

PLATE 76

London Midland and Scottish Railway
High Pressure Compound 4-6-0 No 6399

LMSR No 6399 'Fury' was an experiment doomed to failure from the start. Built to increase the thermal efficiency of the steam locomotive, its designers fell into the age-old trap, which had gaped open since the days of the Liverpool and Manchester and had been emphasised by such nineteenth-century engineers as Pambour and Colburn, and had lost sight of the fact that fuel costs are only one aspect, and not the most important, of a locomotive's total costs. Maintenance (including wages) and capital costs (the latter affected either by high initial price or short life) are altogether more important. Whether or not 'Fury' would have saved any coal would have been irrelevant, for it never ran long enough for this to be ascertained; it offended greatly on other counts, and ultimately settled the matter with a fatal explosion. Of course, research into basic improvement should be continued, and it is interesting to note that although steam is considered played-out on the railways, on the roads the advantages in taming the polluting motor-car by adopting steam technology are regarded as having great possibilities; but practicalities should not be neglected either.

No 6399 was built in 1928, as alike as possible to the LMSR 'Royal Scot' three-cylinder 4-6-0s for purposes of comparison. She had a unique three-part boiler; a relatively conventional short barrel in the fore part of the casing generating steam at 250 psi, and a steam drum above the firebox generating steam at 900 psi. This firebox was not in contact with the fire, but was heated by a small water-tube steam generator, using distilled water and operating in a closed circuit with steam at 1400–1800 psi. Needless to say, this complexity caused serious trouble, even though the theoretical advantages of lessening the temperature gradients in the various parts of the boiler were clear enough. Mechanically the engine was a semi-compound, with 900 psi steam fed to a single HP cylinder and then, augmented by 250 psi steam, to the two outside LP cylinders. Following the accident on trials, the engine was ultimately rebuilt into a modified 'Royal Scot' and as such ran until the early 1960s.

PLATE 77

German State Railways
Class HO2[10]

In the 1920s and 1930s, there was a spate of strange looking, complicated steam engines produced in various parts of the world, each an attempt to improve upon the steam locomotive's comparatively low thermal efficiency. The competing diesel and electric locomotives then being built offered far greater thermal efficiencies on paper, but steam engineers rarely seemed able to evaluate these counter-claims on a strictly comparable basis. The 'over 30 per cent' efficiency of the diesel related to the engine only—by the time that transmission and auxiliary losses had been considered, efficiency was less than 20 per cent. Electrics started off with a power station efficiency rather over 30 per cent, and with transmission losses in the catenary, and in the locomotive, ended down at the diesel level.

What few seem to have realised was that capital charges on these newer and vastly more expensive forms of traction exceeded the unburnt coal costs of the 'wasteful' steam engine, so that full running costs, taking everything into account, for the whole life cycle of each type, did not by any means show steam unfavourably.

In an effort to compete with the diesel in capital cost, complexity, unreliability and fuel saving, engines like the above were tried out, none of them successfully. The German effort was a three-cylinder compound, with one low- and two high-pressure cylinders, *à la* Webb, although all axles were coupled. An incredibly complex, multi-pressure boiler delivered high-pressure steam to two cylinders so small that the pistons were little more than collars on the piston rods, after which it was exhausted into the single LP cylinder. As far as can be verified, the engine never saw regular service: it has been portrayed, typically, sitting in a shed.

PLATE 78

Southern Railway

'Schools' Class 4-4-0

From time to time, in the art of steam locomotive design, an engine would be put together from components drawn from other classes, and the result would amaze all by its magnificent performance. Britain's best steam locomotive, the 9F 2-10-0, was such a collection of standard components, and so was Maunsell's 'Schools' class for the Southern. The boiler was a shortened version of the 'King Arthur' and S15 steam generator – only a bit at the front of the barrel was lopped off, leaving that important organ, the firebox, full size. Below, the four-cylinder 'Lord Nelson' was taken as a basis, with one cylinder, also a coupled axle and its wheels, omitted. The resulting three-cylinder 4-4-0 was the largest and most powerful of its type to run outside the USA, and it is doubtful whether even the bigger American 4-4-0s ever outshone a 'Schools' in performance. Despite the limitations of 42 tons adhesion weight, the 'Schools' rarely experienced trouble in starting, except perhaps from platforms 6 and 7 at London Bridge. They were often allocated full-length expresses of a dozen coaches, weighing well over 350 tons. With these, they would romp down to Bournemouth in two hours, on less than 4 000 gallons of water. This gave an average steaming rate of about 18 000 lb per hour, with a maximum clearly around 25 000, although no fully documented tests appear to have been made with the engines. Smoke-deflecting plates, as seen, were fitted soon after the class appeared, and Bulleid later equipped about half of them with Lemaitre blast pipes and 'dustbin' chimneys. After half the class had been whittled away by withdrawals, the remainder were written off at one swoop by Beeching's accountants on gloomy 31 December 1962.

PLATE 79

Czechoslovakian State Railways
Class 387.0 4-6-2

A new country, sliced out of the Austrian empire after the First World War, Czechoslovakia was fortunate in inheriting an active and thriving locomotive industry, and it was not long before construction of the Austrian types ceased, and native designs began to appear. True, most of the early Czech designs still looked like Austrian engines, but a national standard of design quickly evolved. First of the truly Czech engines were the three-cylindered 'Pacifics' of class 387.0 shown in this painting. Detailing was elegant to a high degree, and although there was, of course, an inside cylinder, the primary motion for the inside valve was derived from an outside return crank mounted on the left trailing crankpin, and seen clearly here. The 387.0 class nominally superseded the earlier Czech 365.0 2-6-2s, which in turn were designed to replace Gölsdorf's splendid 2-6-4 compound express engines, inherited

from Austria. The 387.0 were forerunners of successive three-cylinder passenger classes, 4-8-2, 2-8-4, and 4-8-4T built up to 1955.

All the 'Pacifics' have now been fitted with smoke deflectors, and about half of them with double Kylchap chimneys, while most, if not all, have lost the green livery for an overall black, relieved with the statutory red star on smokebox door, plus red wheels, and whatever trimmings a keen foreman may prescribe as the norm for his shed.

PLATE 80

Chicago, Milwaukee, St. Paul & Pacific Railroad
Class F6 4-6-4

The cumbersome full title of this railroad is a relic of the American 'railway mania', when promoters had only to add '& Pacific' on to their railroad name in order to ensure that everybody bought shares. Unlike many others, the CMStP &P did eventually reach the Pacific coast, but in later days called itself by the shorter, slicker, and more truthful title, The Milwaukee Road: since its centre of gravity was always north and west of Chicago, and its principal main line ran between Chicago and the twin cities of Minneapolis and St Paul.

For the heaviest expresses, the earlier 4-6-2s were supplemented, in 1930–31, with these fine large 4-6-4s, plus a corresponding 4-8-4 mixed traffic design, both sharing the unusual feature of an outside-framed leading bogie. Solid, conventional steam power of the Al Capone era, the F6s showed their capabilities in the 1930s, when the competing Burlington Route introduced a streamlined diesel train-set.

The Milwaukee countered by running steam and conventional stock at competitive schedules, and found it so satisfactory that new, ultra high-speed steam power was designed and built for the new 'Hiawatha' expresses.

The first of these racers were 4-4-2 'Atlantic'-type engines, but as traffic grew, larger 4-6-4 high-speed engines were introduced, a logical development of the engine shown here. These new F7 class put up phenomenal performances, and speeds of 100 mph were normal day-to-day running, not just on a down-hill sprint, but for long level stretches of about 50 miles at a time. Top speeds of 120 mph were common, and the Milwaukee can claim to have been one of the fastest, if not *the* fastest, lines in the world using steam traction.

PLATE 81

Reading Railway
2-10-2 No 3014

These very large 2-10-2s had an interesting history. Between 1917 and 1919 the Philadelphia and Reading Railroad had built, by Baldwin, a series of very large 2-8-8-2 compound 'Mallets' for heavy haulage over gradients as steep as 3 per cent (1 in 33). In the 1930s, there was a decline in the requirement for such large, low-speed power, and steps were taken to increase the usefulness of these engines. Some were altered to simple expansion 'Mallets' and ten suffered a more drastic alteration to 2-10-2s, using the 'Mallet' boiler, slightly shortened, with a new frame rolled in underneath. These proved very successful, so much so that 10 more were later built new to the same design, the engine shown being one of these.

It is strange how Americans had to learn the same lesson twice. This 2-10-2 class resulting from the rebuilding, typified modern operating methods, whereby overall line capacity could be increased by replacing the enormous steam dinosaurs of the 1910 era, capable of hauling immense loads at walking speed, by high horse-power machines which despite having a lower tractive effort were capable of moving lighter trains far faster. When diesels came out, in the late 1940s, the standard designs were low horse-power, high-tractive effort machines which, unless they were used in multiples, took the railroads right back to the unsuperheated, compound 'Mallet' era!

As a result, multiple heading of locomotives, an evil which steam engineers strove long to eliminate, has become the established rule in diesel days, for no builder has yet produced a single diesel which can, unaided, haul the loads of the largest steam power. The evil is mitigated, but by no means avoided, by the possibility of working several diesels with only one crew and multiple-unit control gear.

PLATE 82

Indiana Harbour Belt Railroad
Three cylinder 0-8-0

In the 1920s, a number of American railroads were interested in the possibilities of three-cylinder propulsion. The main advantage claimed, that of reduced piston thrust, was a valid one in the days of rapidly increasing engine dimensions, and but for the development of one-piece cast steel engine beds, (so called as the word 'frame' had implications of beanstalks and matchsticks in this context) which could safely take higher piston-loads, three-cylinder power may have had, from sheer necessity, more application. The big snag, from an American viewpoint, was the inside cylinder and motion. USA enginemen were not accustomed to oiling and otherwise maintaining machinery tucked away between the frames, and such machinery tended to become neglected with consequent trouble and disaster.

Where railroads—only a few—had significant numbers of three-cylinder power, this difficulty was soon overcome as crews became familiarised, but odd experimental engines were soon in disgrace. Another rather nebulous advantage claimed was that there were more exhaust beats per revolution, and that each was softer and less destructive to the firebed. This was equally true for the unsynchronised exhausts of a 'Garratt' or of a simple-expansion 'Mallet' but of course, as speed rose, the exhaust pulses tended to become a near continuous roar, and it mattered little whether the engine had two cylinders, three, or an unsynchronised four.

These IHB 0-8-0s with, as can be seen, a booster on the leading tender bogie, eventually had the centre piston and machinery discarded, cranks quartered, and ended life as normal switchers, although the empty cavern of the centre cylinder, integrally cast in, remained in mute evidence of the engines' former position as the world's most powerful eight-wheeled locomotives.

PLATE 83

Duluth, Missabe and Northern Railroad

0-10-0

Seen against the terraced sides of an opencast iron ore working, this massive, Baker-geared beast, is one of the largest shunting ('switching') locomotives ever built. Surprisingly, US railroads rarely progressed beyond the 0-8-0 for switching duties, even though trains of up to 15 000 long tons had to be handled, with 10 000 tons fairly common on the coal roads. The DM&N's iron ore traffic, the line's staple freight, was undoubtedly the reason behind the acquisition of such heavy shunting power. Apart from its sheer size, the engine had no features of particular interest, although the tender had, at the period of this painting, a booster on the leading bogie. The coupling rods on this tender booster, together with the flexible steam pipe connexions from the locomotive, are clearly visible. Later, this railroad was one of the constituents forming the Duluth, Missabe and Iron Range system, connecting the Minnesota ore workings with the steamers on Lake Superior. The DM&IRR was notable in running the heaviest trains the world has ever seen hauled by a *single locomotive*: 180 or 190 bogie ore hoppers, totalling 19 000 US short tons were an everyday working behind one of the huge Baldwin 'Yellowstone' 2-8-8-4 simple expansion 'Mallets', and such a cavalcade would average 30 mph over the main line section. Today's diesel units have not the tractive capacity of yesterday's massive 'Mallets', and even the largest of those currently produced needed to be worked in multiple units in order to equal the output of a 2-8-8-4. The 0-10-0s featured in the painting lasted well, and were still used in Procter yard, on the lake side, into the late 1950s.

PLATE 84

Halberstadt Blankenburger Railway

2-10-2T

Until 1920, it was generally thought that railways much steeper than about 1 in 25 needed to be worked on the rack and toothed wheel, or equivalent system, such as the Fell centre rail. Indeed, the steepest section of the Halberstadt-Blankenburg line, on a gradient of 1 in 16.66 (6 per cent) had been operating as a rack line.

After the First World War, German engineers decided that this line could be worked by adhesion, provided that sufficient power was available; and Borsig, of Berlin, built four squat, massive, 2-10-2Ts to test the theory. They were named, *Mammut*, *Elch*, *Wisent* and *Buffel*, appropriate names meaning 'Mammoth', 'Elk', 'Bison' and 'Buffalo', conjuring up visions of massive power unusual on a main-line railway of that date, let alone a private, short line. The design included very small driving wheels; and 'oversquare' cylinders, of diameter greater than stroke were proportioned to give the maximum tractive effort allowable by adhesion, at 65 per cent cut-off. In practice, these engines could lift about 200 tons up the gradient, at substantially higher speeds than the rack engines they displaced. As a result, a number of rack lines in Germany were converted to adhesion working, including sections of the State-owned Reichsbahn, such as the Höllental line in the Black Forest, which was still running passenger trains up 1 in 18 gradients behind massive 2-10-2Ts in 1959.

The Halberstadt line is now in East Germany, and its four 2-10-2Ts have been taken over by the State and renumbered 95 6676 to 95 6679. They were recently reported as intact, but were kept only as reserves for the larger ex-Prussian T20 class.

PLATE 85

Norwegian State Railways
49a Class 2-8-4 No 463 'Dovregubben'

These remarkable machines were the last and largest locomotives to be designed and built in Norway. They compare with the 4-8-0 compounds of 1915-21 built for the Oslo-Bergen line (see plate No 64), and some fair-sized 0-10-0 and 2-10-0 freight engines of the same period fitted with counter-pressure braking. By the mid-1930s the need was felt for some larger engines, particularly on the section of the Olso-Trondheim main line north of Dombas, where the railway climbed over the high and desolate Dovre Fjell, and where the maximum axleload was restricted to no more than 16·25 tons. In 1935 Thunes of Oslo built three 2-8-4 four-cylinder compounds, which incorporated a modern front end and managed to combine a power output of 2 600 hp with the severe weight limits. The first locomotive was unofficially named 'Dovregubben', or Dovre Giant. Four more were built during the war (two in Germany), and they remained

rulers of the mountain until the Dovre line was converted to diesel in the early 1960s, when weight restrictions prevented their being used elsewhere. Thus in Norway, as in so many other countries, the most advanced steam engines were among the earliest casualties of progress; older machines still having as much as another decade of service.

One or two details of the design were surprisingly anachronistic for 1935; notably perhaps the use of a rear bogie with inside bearings. However the generous Norwegian loading gauge allowed adequate room for a large ashpan and side dampers without encroaching on the space for springs and bearings. The frameless Vanderbilt tender, widely used in the USA, was uncommon in Europe; in this case the tender had the notably un-American extra of retractable wooden covers over the bunker to prevent the coal from freezing (otherwise quite possible even

in summer). To assist in rounding curves, the leading radial wheels and the leading coupled wheels were mounted in a Zara truck, forming a separate bogie frame (with an extra knuckle joint in the coupling rods); an Italian design feature also fairly uncommon outside its native land.

PLATE 86

London, Midland and Scottish Railway:
Class 8P 4-6-2

Little doubt here, but this may well have been Britain's finest express engine. Gresley's A4s were officially faster, downhill, but could not approach the power output at speed of a 'Duchess'. The highest output recorded with steam on a British railway was over 3 300 ihp behind one of these Stanier machines, observed while climbing Shap at speed with 600 tons behind the tender.

The background of these fine engines was hardly one to inspire confidence in their eventual success. Arriving at Derby from Swindon, as the new Chief Mechanical Engineer, Stanier found drawings, and even components for Fowler's ill-fated compound 4-6-2, stillborn and ousted by the 'Royal Scot' 4-6-0. Good though the 'Scot' was, it was no match for Gresley's famous 'Pacifics' on the competing East Coast route, and Stanier produced a highly successful stop gap by grafting a Great Western 'King' front end on to the fossilised bones of Fowler's compound 4-6-2, thus creating the 'Princess Royal' class.

This pointed in the right direction, and was completely redesigned as the officially termed 'Princess Coronation' class, generally known as 'Duchesses'. There was only one thing wrong with the 'Duchesses' – they were too few in number; and right to the end of steam on the West Coast route to Scotland, smaller engines were seen more often than big, either struggling single-headed, or coping double-headed, with consequent waste of fuel or manpower respectively.

PLATE 87

Northern Pacific Railway
Class Z9 4-6-6-4

Amongst the finest developments of American steam power, in latter days, was the 4-6-6-4 type high-speed simple expansion 'Mallet'. Originally conceived by the design engineers of the Union Pacific Railroad, and the American Locomotive Company, these successfully combined the haulage capacities of the earlier, small-wheeled 'Mallets' with the speed capabilities of a 4-8-2. As a fast freight engine they were surpassed only by their development, the 4-8-8-4, and this was employed only by the Union Pacific itself.

The 4-6-6-4, on the other hand, was adopted by a number of railroads, both in the West and the East, and in addition to fast freight haulage, their engines were regularly assigned to passenger duties over difficult mountain routes, especially to the Union Pacific. The Northern Pacific engines, of which there were 50, had fireboxes designed to burn the same low-grade coal as their 2-8-8-4s (see plate No 74), and the grate area was correspondingly larger than other designs of this type—slightly larger in fact than the UP 'Big Boy'. The painting shows a Z9 in passenger service, evidently amongst the coniferous forests of Oregon or Washington states, climbing hard with the exhaust beat of each unit changing continuously in and out of phase in that fascinating, syncopated, rhythm which is the marching tune of simple expansion 'Mallets' and 'Garratts' everywhere.

PLATE 88

Chesapeake and Ohio Railway
Class H7 2-8-8-2

The massive 'Mallets' were the first large scale application of simple expansion to the 'Mallet' chassis in the US. They were not the very first, however, for the Pennsylvania had preceded them with two experimental locomotives, whilst both Russia and South Africa had tried out simple Mallets prior to the H7's introduction. These great engines can still claim to have put the simple 'Mallet' on the map, paving the way for the developments that were to follow, and it is interesting to realise that their introduction was originally a matter of necessity rather than choice. The main C&O artery from the West Virginia coalfields to the East Coast, traversed the Allegheny mountain range via a tunnel of small cross section, and when loads greater than the capacity of the existing 2-6-6-2 compound 'Mallets' were planned, it was found that clearances were too tight to accommodate the LP cylinders of the

corresponding larger eight-coupled compound. Accordingly, the simple was designed and built, and successfully handled 10 000-ton trains over the main line for a number of years.

Passing behind the Mallet, is one of the engines which supplanted them, a 2-10-4 of lesser tractive effort but substantially greater hp, which revolutionised the line's carrying capacity by bowling these immense trains along at high speeds. With 5 ft 9 in driving wheels against the 'Mallet's' 4 ft 9 in, 6 000 against 4 000 hp, the 2-10-4s ruled until, before dieselisation, an even greater 'Mallet', a high-speed 2-6-6-6 of 7 500 hp took over as King of the Alleghenies.

PLATE 89

Union Pacific Railroad

'Challenger' 4-6-6-4 and 'Big Boy' 4-8-8-4

One of the world's most exciting railways is, and was, the Union Pacific. One of the two lines to connect in the first American transcontinental link, at Promontory, Utah, in 1869, the UP has since then usually been in the forefront of American railroad practice and operation.

Traffic since 1900 has tended to be both fast and heavy, which, coupled with fairly steep gradients on some sections, necessitated locomotives of exceptional power. The final development of these were the two types shown double-headed here which, with a large modern passenger 4-8-4 made a trio of truly eminent designs with which the Company ended its steam operations in 1959.

The 4-6-6-4 and 4-8-8-4 were each articulated on the Mallet principle, although using high pressure steam in all four cylinders. Wheel diameter was 5 ft 7 in and 5 ft 8 in, a slight and puzzling difference in the two designs, either of which size was adequate for the 80 mph speeds they were called upon to attain, and for dealing with mile-long freights weighing over 3 000-tons. Some idea of their size and capacity may be made by comparing each with a corresponding British design—the 'Challenger' is equal to three BR 'Britannias', and the 'Big Boy' to four! Thus, on the train shown, there is the equivalent of seven 'Britannias'.

In later days, double heading of these monsters became a regular practice, due to heavier and heavier loadings, and the 'Big Boys' were kept on main-line freight right to the end, when, pulled out of storage for the autumn grain rush, they were still capable of outperforming the standard four-unit diesels.

The 'Challengers' were used on passenger work, in addition to their more usual freight duties, and were regularly assigned to such name trains as their namesake, the 'Challenger'. 'Big Boys', on the other hand, saw little passenger service, mainly as there were no passenger trains sufficiently heavy to require their immense, 7 000 dbhp output.

(*NB This plate also appears on the dust jacket of this book.*)

PLATE 90

Norfolk and Western Railway
Class Y5 2-8-8-2

The last major stronghold of steam locomotion in the US was the Norfolk and Western, whose principal traffic consisted of coal. For hauling this, various series of compound 2-8-8-2s were constructed, all based on the Government-instituted 'United States Railroad Administration' set of standard designs during and soon after the First World War. With its superb servicing facilities, the N&W recorded higher monthly engine-mileages with its steam power than many railroads obtained from their diesels, and as a result, new steam engines were being built at the Company's Roanoake shops until the mid-1950s.

However, all good things come to an end, and with most of its shares held by outside interests, this highly profitable railway was pressurised a few years later into abandoning its steam policy. Internal-combustion engine manufacturers were supposed to make the profits—not the railroads! Amongst the fine and powerful locomotives consigned with indecent haste to the scrap heap were the compound 2-8-8-2s of various classes, such as the Y5 shown here. Trains of over 10 000 short tons were normal loading for one of these monsters over the main line from Roanoke to Newport News, where the coal was shipped for transport by sea.

PLATE 91

Russian Railways
Class P36 4-8-4

These imposing engines were the last new steam passenger class designed and built in Soviet Russia before the abandonment of steam. Despite the difference in ideological outlook, the later Russian steam types were borrowed extensively from USA practice, and the 4-8-4 was perhaps the most American of the lot. From Boxpok wheels to skyline casing to 12-wheeled tender, painted in the right colours, few Americans would have noticed anything amiss had a P36 headed a Southern Pacific 'Daylight' express through California. However, the green livery was more English than American, and someone may have looked askance at the Soviet star on the smokebox door. Essentially an all-purpose passenger engine, the P36 was lighter in axle loading than the previous 'Josef Stalin' 2-8-4, which also included numerous American features. Overhead passes a freight train headed by an SO18 2-10-0,

a medium power engine descended from the ubiquitous E class 0-10-0. Certain of the same basic class, with lighter axle load, were classed SO17, and large numbers of the type, built for operating in the dry areas of southern Russia, were equipped with condensing apparatus.

PLATE 92

Pennsylvania Railroad
Class T1 4-4-4-4

The T1 class was a magnificent concept which did not quite come off, due to a mixture of defective detailing and inertia in the development stages. The basic idea of a 'Duplex' drive, ie two complete sets of machinery, uncoupled, but mounted on a single rigid frame under one boiler, originated in France, in the 1860s when M Petiet, of the CF du Nord, built a number of extraordinary 0-6-6-0Ts for heavy coal traffic, plus a couple of even weirder 0-2-6-2-0Ts for passenger work. In modern days, Baldwin, fearful of the heavy piston thrusts and out-of-balance forces borne by the largest US steam power, suggested the 'Duplex' arrangement as a palliative, halving the individual piston thrust for an engine of given power.

This was 'old hat', of course, in Britain and Europe, where engines with two inside and two outside cylinders had long been successfully used, but as crank axles and inside cylinders were feared and distrusted by American enginemen, all cylinders had to be positioned outside. This posed a problem of coupling the two units, as the rear cylinders were in the way. There were three alternative methods of achieving this, inside coupling rods with *two* crank axles, gears, or chain and sprockets, all ruled out as impractical. Hence, Baldwin proposed the uncoupled version, alienating most motive power men who argued, rightly as it turned out, that adhesion would suffer. Only two railroads took the bait, B&O who built one themselves, and PRR who persisted and tried 79 duplexes, of four different types, before giving up.

The T1s, 52 strong, were the most numerous and the least successful. Adhesion problems were paramount, whilst poppet valves with inaccessible cam boxes upset the maintenance staff. Once on the move, they could run, and although no authenticated records exist, they were possibly the fastest steam locomotives ever built—there are stories of them running for miles with the speedometer needle jammed tight against the stop at 130 mph, and whilst this seems likely of such an engine, it cannot be verified. Designed to haul 880 US tons at 100 mph one recorded 6 552 ihp on Altoona test plant.

(continued from page 7)
dead, are probably no longer in existence, as, no doubt, is the case of the painting *The Bangkok Mail*, once owned by the great German firm of Hanomag.

Among what survived in England, however, besides notes for projected articles on locomotives, were files galore of completed chapters or condensed notes bearing witness to what he hoped to achieve. There was, for instance, begun many years before but added to from time to time, the plan, some developed parts and drawings for what could have been his chief work, entitled simply *The Locomotive*.

Latterly, conscious that he might not have a long life, he had concentrated more on a work that was to be entitled *Locomotive Design as a Fine Art*, or possibly, *The Fascination of the Railway Engine*, in which the aim would be to "bridge the gulf between the 'story-book' and the technical manual".

In this he set out to explain his idea of the aesthetic appeal of the locomotive, "in which the cylinder is combined with the square and the circle in different aspects . . . a fascinating matrix of cylinders bonded together with rectilinear framework." In additional clarification of his viewpoint there was one chapter entitled 'The ugly locomotive.' For the painting of what he called his "Locomotive *Portraits*" he divided the picture into three parts. First, the locomotive, "itself being a work of art", should be painted in full detail and with perfect accuracy, with such modifications made to the original design at any time that had improved its looks. Secondly, what he called "connected features"—rolling-stock, track, signals etc.—were to be painted in less detail and, thirdly, the background, in still less, so as not to distract attention. The background, however, should be "arranged" to suit the design, rhythm and composition of the picture and, while being typical of the scenery

or locale in which the engine could normally be seen, was not necessarily to be the picture of one actual spot. The colour-pattern of the painting "starts of course from the fixed, actual colouring of the engine". Colour and shading could be slightly enhanced and reflections minimized, to bring out points of design.

To meet criticisms that his engines looked too much as though newly "hatched" from the shops and less picturesque or lifelike than had they shown more dirt and signs of service, he wrote: "The engine itself is to be clean and not begrimed", and as it were, "a portrait in best clothes rather than in an old gardening suit". Criticism of too minute detail he countered with the note: "*cf* Holbein, Van Eyck, every bead, every thread." In short, his locomotive portraits were evidently to be painted in the tradition of the Old Masters rather than in that of the Impressionists or Picasso.

Obituary notices spoke of Hugh Le Fleming as "invariably sociable and cheerful," "the most approachable of men", "a valued and knowledgeable friend", while Dr P. Ransome Wallis, with whom he went on several trips, described him as "always the most courteous, interesting and stimulating companion". He was also the most modest of men and would, one knows, have been astonished at the tributes paid to him after his death. Above all, would he have been pleased and happy that The Institution of Mechanical Engineers should have considered reproducing the portraits of his beloved steam engines.

R Le F

Narrator's Notes

In preparing the captions, or narratives for these paintings by the late Hugh Le Fleming, I have avoided the temptation to enter into lengthy technical descriptions. Firstly, of course, such details are readily available in both book and journal form, and there seems no point in simply repeating information accessible elsewhere. Secondly, the paintings are all 'alive', and redolent with the character of the locomotives themselves, and of the railways upon which they operated, something no list of dimensions and accessories can convey. Thus, each has been described in the easy manner which the artist used himself, when showing his paintings—pointing out technical and historical features of interest, but not elaborating upon them. Many matters set down in the narratives in the present work were thus recounted to the writer by Hugh Le Fleming directly.

A.E.D.

Acknowledgements

The originals of Plates 2, 3, 5, 6, 12, 16, 23, 25, 30, 58, 61, 68, 73, 77, 88, and 91 are the property of Mrs R. le Fleming, and the original of Plate 89 is the property of Lord Garnock. The Institution of Mechanical Engineers acknowledges with thanks the consent of the owners of these paintings to their reproduction. All remaining plates are from originals donated to The Institution of Mechanical Engineers by Mrs. le Fleming.